# THE MAKING OF
# KING KONG

## The Official Guide to the Motion Picture

# JENNY WAKE

Motion Picture Screenplay by Fran Walsh & Philippa Boyens & Peter Jackson

Based on a Story by Merian C. Cooper and Edgar Wallace

POCKET BOOKS

New York   London   Toronto   Sydney

POCKET BOOKS, an imprint of
Simon & Schuster UK Ltd
Africa House,
64–78 Kingsway
London WC2B 6AH

Unit photography by Pierre Vinet. Provided by and © 2005 Universal Studios.
Photographs on p. 26 of Jeremy Bennett and Gus Hunter © Matt Mueller & Iva Lenard.
Screenshot on p. 180 from *Peter Jackson's King Kong: The Official Game Of The Movie*
provided by and © 2005 Ubisoft Entertainment.
Silverback gorilla photo on p. 188 © OSF/A. Plumtre.
Photograph on p. 206 of Matt Aitken © Matt Mueller & Iva Lenard.
Photograph of Park Road Post on p. 216 © Stephen Goodenough.

ISBN: 1–4165–0257–2

This Pocket Books trade paperback edition December 2005

10 9 8 7 6 5 4 3 2 1

POCKET BOOKS and colophon are registered trademarks of
Simon & Schuster

*Designed by Ruth Lee Mui*

Manufactured in the United States of America

# CONTENTS

# THE MAKING OF
# KING KONG

Filmmaker Peter Jackson.

One night, when Peter Jackson was nine years old, he saw the original *King Kong* in flickering black and gray on television. The classic movie made him cry—and set him on the path to a brilliant film career.

"That moment of seeing *King Kong* was the moment I decided I wanted to become a filmmaker," says the multi-award-winning director, thirty-four years later. "I wanted to do what the makers of *King Kong* did. I wanted to bring to life stories and adventures and creatures that couldn't possibly be done any other way than through making a movie."

It is late afternoon on an autumn day, 2005, in Wellington, New Zealand, and postproduction on Peter's remake of *King Kong* is in full swing. He snatches a few moments between meetings to lie back on the window seat in the farmhouse-style kitchen at the headquarters of WingNut Films (the production company he co-owns with screenwriter Fran Walsh) and reflect on the magic of the original *King Kong*.

"It was the perfect piece of escapism," he says. "When I was nine, it swept me away. I was transported into this amazing world and this adventure." Central to the adventure was Kong, the giant ape, portrayed initially as a monster but bit by bit transformed into a sympathetic creature. "I was sobbing by the time Kong died at the end of the movie. It was the perfect blend of mysterious adventure with a story that touched your heart.

"People go to the movies for different reasons, and everybody is different in what they like and dislike. I love escapism. I think movies should let you experience things that you can't experience in your real life, and going to a lost island and finding it inhabited by dinosaurs and a huge gorilla—to me, that was just the perfect escapist entertainment."

# A VISIONARY FILMMAKER

The original *King Kong* was made in 1933 by Ernest B. Schoedsack and Merian C. Cooper. It starred Fay Wray as the beauty who captures the hearts of both the beast Kong and the sailor Jack Driscoll, played by Bruce Cabot. In the 1930s, America was in the grips of the Great Depression. The Empire State Building had just opened, little was known about mountain gorillas, and animation was in its infancy. *King Kong* wowed Depression-era audiences with its savage beasts and derring-do and has continued to move audiences to tears through the decades.

*King Kong*'s monsters were created by special effects genius Willis O'Brien. O'Brien had pioneered a technique known as stop-motion animation, for which he filmed creature models one frame at a time, repositioning them slightly between each exposure. When the film was played back at normal speed, the creatures appeared to be moving. O'Brien's Kong stood eighteen inches tall. It had a steel skeleton with ball-and-socket joints. It was padded with foam rubber and covered with rabbit fur. Frame by frame, it battled dinosaurs with thrilling ferocity, ruthlessly dashed sailors and hapless New Yorkers to their deaths, fell hopelessly in love with young actress Ann Darrow, and made a heroic last stand against civilization from the top of New York's Empire State Building.

To today's audiences, accustomed to digital effects, O'Brien's pioneering stop-motion animation looks quaintly artificial, yet Kong still springs to life as a character. "The power of the original *King Kong* didn't dwell in how realistic the effects are. It's the magic of the film," says Peter. "It's the sum of all the parts. It doesn't matter that you can see the magician performing the tricks. It's the quality of the tricks that has the effect on you."

Being able to see how the magic was done on *King Kong* allowed Peter to have a go at it himself. "In a way, the artifice is still what's exciting about stop-motion. It excites you about the possibilities of filmmaking. You're bringing inanimate objects to life and you can invest them with a personality. Certainly it was possible even as a kid to do the same thing. There are a huge number of filmmakers, special effects people, makeup artists, who owe their careers to the original *King Kong*. That one movie has, I think, started more people on a career in filmmaking than any other film ever."

Peter's own first steps toward a film career involved lots of plasticine and his parents' Super 8 movie camera. At age nine, inspired by *King Kong*, he started sculpting dinosaurs and other little monsters and moving them around. For a year or two he experimented with the camera and made various short Super 8 films.

Then he hatched a plan to actually remake *King Kong*. "I would have been about twelve or thirteen by that time. I made a model of King Kong, for which I used a fur stole that my mother had in her wardrobe. I'd never seen her wear it in my whole life, so I managed to get her to part with it, and I trimmed off the fur. I made a little rubber King Kong with wire inside him, and I glued on the fur off Mum's fur stole. I made a cardboard model of the top of the Empire State Building, and my mum donated an old bedsheet, which I painted. I stretched it out and pinned it up on a board and I painted a backdrop of the Manhattan skyline. I put my Empire State Building in front of it and did a little bit of stop-motion animation with Kong. I started to do a little bit of jungle too. I made some plastic trees and I had a little stop-motion plasticine brontosaurus sort of grazing on the trees.

"I didn't get very far. The filming took a long, long time to do, but was probably no more than thirty or forty seconds. I had a lot of fun building the models, but I realized that trying to do a remake of *King Kong* was a little bit ambitious. I still have that film somewhere. I haven't seen it for years, but I've got all of my old films in a box. And I have that Kong. He's very deteriorated now, but he's still in one piece."

Throughout his teenage years, Peter dreamed of someday becoming a special effects man. "I didn't really have any ambitions to be a director as such," he says. "I guess I didn't really know what directors did when I was young, but I knew what special effects guys did, so for a long time I wanted to do stop-motion as a career. But then, as I did little tests and made short movies, I realized that a lot of the fun is making up ideas for stories and telling stories through film and learning how the camera angles and the cutting all go together to make a movie. I realized that the most fun is if you direct the movie, and that a career in being a special effects person would ultimately be a bit frustrating because I wouldn't be telling the stories that I wanted to do. So it took me till I was in my twenties before I realized that being a director was what I really wanted to do."

Peter's first feature film was *Bad Taste*, a hilariously grisly horror-comedy about aliens set on harvesting fresh human meat for their intergalactic fast-food franchise. It was filmed on weekends over four years, with a handful of Peter's best friends acting as cast and crew. Peter, who was working as a photo engraver for a local newspaper at the time, saved every cent he could to buy film stock and materials and made his own props, special effects makeup, camera rigs, and pretty much everything else he needed, in his parents' garage. Eventually the New Zealand Film Commission provided funding for postproduction, and in 1988 *Bad Taste* splattered onto screens around the world, starting with the Cannes Film Festival.

"Peter is a very unique director because he has

Richard Taylor with Peter Jackson on the set of *King Kong*.

never had to serve his time on other people's film sets," says Richard Taylor, Peter's longtime friend and business partner. "He decided one day he'd become a film director and so became a film director."

Richard and Peter first met when Peter was directing *Bad Taste* and Richard was working as a model-maker on a television commercial. By chance, a mutual friend invited Peter to visit during production of the commercial. "I had heard rumors of this filmmaker up in Pukerua Bay making this alien movie, so I went over and chatted to him," says Richard. The meeting would ultimately lead to career partnerships, award-winning movies, and the fulfillment of dreams.

At that time, Richard and his partner Tania Rodger were building puppets in the back room of their home and dreaming of one day creating a substantial special effects facility. "Over the next years

Tania and I spent much time in Peter's company . . . every evening we'd spend time together talking about Ray Harryhausen movies, and talking about *King Kong* a lot."

Richard and Tania provided puppets, miniatures, and gore effects for Peter's next movies, *Meet the Feebles* and *Braindead* (aka *Dead Alive*). Their friendship led in 1994 to the formation of Weta, the award-winning special effects company co-owned by Richard, Tania, Peter, and film editor Jamie Selkirk. With the release of *Heavenly Creatures*, *Forgotten Silver*, and *The Frighteners*, Weta grew and diversified into the realm of digital effects, eventually becoming two companies, Weta Workshop and Weta Digital.

"Making films is our passion," says Richard, "so we will build the facilities we need for a particular film, as much as we can afford to, by mortgaging everything else again to get the facilities built. We

1996 Triceratops creature concept by Christian Rivers.

1996 Kong face study, ready for mold making.

want to get the films made at the best level we can, so we grin and bear it, hang on for dear life."

It was Universal Studios that initially came to Peter with the idea of doing *King Kong*. "In 1996 we were halfway through *The Frighteners*," recalls Peter. "An executive at Universal who was working with us on *The Frighteners* suddenly called one day and said that they were looking at properties that the studio owned that they wanted to develop in the future and did we have any interest in some of their ideas. He mentioned two or three titles and one was *King Kong*. I nearly fell off my chair!" Peter laughs. "I said, 'It's my favorite film! You really want to do a version of *King Kong*? Wow! Yeah, sure!'"

Peter and his partners swung into action. Peter and Fran wrote a script, and Richard and Tania contracted extra staff. "We hired a fairly large crew," says Richard Taylor. "We invested in more digital equip-

Dominic Taylor fine-tunes a pneumatic Kong hand mechanism in 1996.

ment, set up the facility here at the workshop ready to take on the body of work, and launched into the design and preproduction phase."

Bernie Wrightson, American comic-book artist, creature designer, and illustrator, flew to Wellington to help conceptualize the world of Kong and Skull Island. "We did hundreds of illustrations, and dozens and dozens of conceptual sculptures, designing around Kong and the creatures," says Richard. "It was a very delightful and enjoyable time. We were on our first big international feature film and there was a great feeling of euphoria and excitement."

To bring the creatures of Skull Island to life, the plan was to use a combination of stop-motion animation, animatronics, and digital effects. Stop-animation armatures were built for the brontosaurs, tyrannosaurs, Kong, and the raptors and fleshed out with foam latex. Animatronic versions of their heads were planned for close-ups, and work began on a full-size animatronic creature. "In the original script, there was an attack on Sumatra by some giant crocodiles," says Richard, "and we had started sculpting a full-size body and head for this sequence."

A large-scale miniature of the whole of Skull Island was built, from which other miniatures were being planned. Visual effects teams at Weta Digital were working on dinosaur walk cycles, researching techniques for creating Kong's fur, and modeling the whole of New York digitally, building by building.

Six months into preproduction, Universal Studios shelved the plan to remake *King Kong*, after a string of monster movies underperformed at the box office.

As he remembers it, it was three thirty on a Tuesday afternoon when Fran Walsh phoned Weta Workshop with the bad news. Richard recalls, "Pete was with Fran, but was too upset, so Fran called us on his behalf. I went down to the workshop, gathered the crew together, and told them. There were tears and sadness. We felt that we had finally got our chance to prove ourselves and do an international picture of great esteem, and to have lost it was desperate for us at the time."

Most worrying was how to find employment for all the digital artists who had been contracted to work on the project for the next two years. Thankfully, director Robert Zemeckis, who had earlier teamed with Peter and his partners for *The Frighteners*, offered Weta Digital some effects work on the movie *Contact*. "That was a great grace and let us move on," says Richard. "But all credit to Universal, because they stayed with Pete, watched *The Lord of the Rings* unfold, and came back with *King Kong* when the time was more right. They were correct ultimately—we did need to let it go [at that time]. We firmly believe we can do a beautiful job of it today, where I question if we could have back then."

With *King Kong* on the shelf, Peter turned his attention to securing a studio deal to turn J. R. R. Tolkien's trilogy, *The Lord of the Rings*, into a series of movies. In December 2001, *The Lord of the Rings: The Fellowship of the Ring* premiered worldwide to critical acclaim and blockbuster box-office success, as did *The Lord of the Rings: The Two Towers* in December 2002, and *The Lord of the Rings: The Return of the King* in 2003. The trilogy won multiple awards for Peter, Fran, Richard, and others who worked on the films, and catapulted Peter to the very top of Hollywood's A-list of directors.

"It was really Universal killing our 1996 version of *Kong* that propelled us into *The Lord of the Rings*—which in hindsight was obviously a good thing," says Peter, laughing. "We've ended up making everything in the right order, so in a funny kind of way fate's been kind to us. Coming back to *King Kong* now, we've been able to apply everything we learnt from *Lord of the Rings* as filmmakers, and so it's a better time to make *King Kong* now than it would have been in 1996."

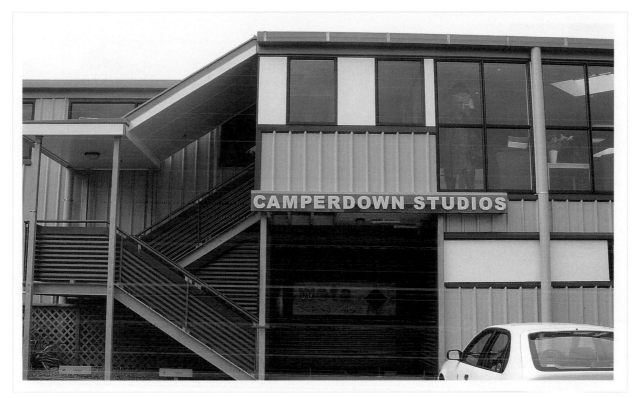

The entrance to Weta Workshop.

*The Lord of the Rings* trilogy took seven and a half years to make, giving Peter and his partners the opportunity to develop a stronger infrastructural base for their moviemaking empire initially based at Camperdown Studios.

Camperdown is a rambling set of interconnected buildings with a colorful history that Richard can recite in great detail, right down to the spot where his mum's lawyer's wife was born. It was a derelict site when Richard and Tania, out for a bike ride, spotted the For Sale sign. It had been a pharmaceutical factory ten years earlier and, before that, a battery factory, a GI intern hospital, and a psychiatric hospital. The friends bought the building for a song. It would turn out to be a first step toward developing all the resources they would eventually need to produce films as big as *King Kong* or *The Lord of the Rings* trilogy.

The quiet suburb of Miramar, Wellington, seems an unlikely setting for a complete collection of cutting-edge film facilities, but is now home to Weta Workshop, Weta Digital, Stone Street Studios, a motion capture stage, Weta Productions (a television production arm), Weta Collectibles, Weta Tenzan Chain Maille (a chain mail manufacturing company), and Weta Publishing. The most recent additions to the film facilities dotted around Miramar include Park Road Post—a state-of-the-art postproduction facility designed and lavishly decorated in the style of architect Frank Lloyd Wright—and a massive new soundstage, dubbed Kong Stage, at Stone Street Studios.

"Today we feel much more adequate to realize a great piece of American pop culture in a suitable way," says Richard. "We've learnt a lot since 1996. Half of our careers have passed since then. We've grown up, and Peter's got greater clarity on what he saw the world of Kong to be. The script is tighter and more dynamic. We've grown more mature and longer

8

Peter Jackson behind the camera.

in the tooth, so we feel that we can bring a much more sophisticated level of design to it."

The version of *King Kong* now in production is radically different from the version that would have been made in 1996. "It was a very simple action-adventure film," says Peter. "It had some of the action sequences that we have today; it didn't very have much of the character development. It didn't have much going on in its heart. . . . It was very over-the-top, and it reveled in its outrageousness in a way. For the film that we're making now, we completely rewrote the script.

"There's no doubt that *The Lord of the Rings* had a huge influence on the way that we ultimately rewrote *Kong*, by making it a little bit more real at its heart, making the characters more real, and making the dynamics between characters more centered and more focused. One lesson that we learnt with *The Lord of the Rings* was that the best way to tackle fantasy is to make it as realistic as you possibly can. No matter what the fantasy is, make the characters and emotions as real as they can be. Our 1996 *King Kong* knew it was a fantasy film and didn't make any attempt to be real."

That's not to say that the 2005 *King Kong* will delve into heavier themes. "We didn't want to over-invest it with too much baggage, too many messages and themes and weighty stuff," Peter says. "There aren't very many what I'd call old-fashioned action-adventures made anymore now. And that's what *King*

*Kong* is—it's sheer escapist entertainment. You can go watch the movie and be swept away to another place, another time, for two hours."

Peter regrets that youngsters no longer watch older classics such as the original *King Kong*. "There is a generation of kids today who have very little patience for watching a film that's in black and white, and of course, *King Kong* has got old effects and old styles of scriptwriting and acting. So to take that great story and to remake it so that it's accessible to kids, I think is a good thing to do.

"The original film will still be there. There's nothing that we're doing that's going to threaten the original film. It's a classic film and will always remain so."

Perhaps with the rise of a new generation of filmmakers, there will be some who say they are making movies because they were inspired by Peter Jackson's *King Kong*. If so, Peter will be delighted: "There is that continuum which I think is very important. You're hoping when you make films that there's some nine- or ten-year-old kid out there who's going to become a filmmaker in twenty years because of the film that you've made."

For now, though, Peter's focus is simply on making a movie that he himself would love to see. "But I'm not so much making this film for the adult me," he says. "I'm making it for the Peter that was nine years old once, who for the first time saw the original *King Kong*."

Adrien Brody as playwright Jack Driscoll, writing in his tiger's cage.

Right at the outset, Peter Jackson decided to set his version of *King Kong* in 1933, the year of the original movie.

"It had to be 1933 so I could do the biplanes," he says, laughing. "You can't in your heart call it a remake of *King Kong* without having him fighting biplanes on the Empire State Building. You just can't. That is such an iconic image of *King Kong*. When Universal approached us about doing the film, that was the only condition that I set. I was absolutely adamant that I didn't want *Kong* to be set in the modern world."

The earlier era also lends a little more plausibility to the film's central premise: "It's kind of important that you can believe that there is an island that's not been discovered yet, that is uncharted—that you could come across Skull Island and that it is inhabited by these beasts. In 1933, it was the tail end of that age of exploration and discovery when there were still a couple of dark corners in the world, a couple of places where the atlas hadn't quite been filled in yet."

Peter and partner Fran Walsh had written an early-draft script back in 1996, but they opted for a fresh start and invited screenwriter Philippa Boyens, with whom they had written the screenplays for *The Lord of the Rings* trilogy, to work with them on a new script for *King Kong*.

Peter screened the 1933 film for Philippa. "I sort of got it, but I didn't love it," she recalls. "But I did love the storytelling, and I loved Fay Wray as Ann. And what I did see when I watched it with Peter was how much *he* loved it, and how much he understood it."

The three were still embroiled in completing *The Return of the King* when ideas for scenes and characters started brewing. "Even if you're not writing, you're beginning to get a handle on the story," says Philippa. "I'll go over in the morning and have a cup of tea with Fran, she will have been talking to Pete, she'll tell me about it, we'll have a conversation. Then we just sat down and started outlining. I remember Fran saying, 'We have to start thinking about the relationship between Kong and Ann.' Stuff was beginning to formulate for her."

Central to the Kong/Ann relationship was the perplexing question of why the huge beast does not simply destroy her, as he has apparently done before. The answer came in a flash of inspiration in a plane somewhere over the Pacific Ocean, when Fran and Peter were on a business trip to Los Angeles.

"They were having a meeting with Universal, and we hadn't done enough work on it because of *Return of the King*," Philippa explains. "So Fran, in her inimitable way, sketched out an outline for the Kong/Ann story on the plane going over

# A CLASSIC STORY

there. Give her a bit of peace and quiet and that incredible brain will start ticking over. And she saw this image of this girl dancing in front of this gorilla, and that gave her this thought that maybe Ann's a dancer. She loved the idea of this gorilla not killing Ann because he has engaged with her. And that was a single, simple image that we all responded to. And then I think it was Pete who said, 'I love that idea, what about vaudeville?'"

Even before the script was completed, Naomi Watts was invited to play the central role of down-on-her-luck actress Ann Darrow. "We knew it had to be someone we loved, who could help us define that character," says Philippa. "Her spirit and her energy and, as it turns out, her incredible humor were all going to feed into creating this character."

Casting and character development typically go hand in hand for the writers: "Suddenly you think: Englehorn's a German name—what about making him German? Oh, okay, so the *Venture* crew should be quite international. We liked the idea that this American filmmaker, with an American writer and stars and assistant, end up on this ship which is kind of a United Nations. All sorts of things start the storytelling process—little threads of this, conversations about that."

Extensive research and a multitude of reference materials enriched the scriptwriting. The writers studied gorillas, looked at documentary films about New York in the 1930s, watched movies set during the Great Depression, and researched tramp steamers. They talked endlessly about the original movie and what was it exactly that made it so good. They investigated different civilizations, tribes, ancient architecture and delved into archaeological books about Cambodia, Angkor Wat, and Sumatra.

Naomi Watts as Ann Darrow.

"You pick things up and you learn things, and it helps," says Peter. "Not a lot of it makes it into the movie particularly, but you learn a lot so that you understand the world that you are setting the film in."

The pictorial reference materials also gave Peter ideas for images he would like to see on-screen. Certain shots of New York in the film are faithful recreations of photographs from the thirties era. "There's a great photo of a street with a huge bridge, one of the bridges just towering at the end of the street, which I always loved, so there's a shot in the film which is an exact copy of that photo. You definitely get inspired."

Peter, Fran, and Philippa all have a hand in writing scenes and dialogue, although Fran and Philippa do the lion's share of the rewrites. "We sit down together, write together or write separately, but Pete's always still got his eye on the overall story," says Philippa. "He often gives actors lines when he's shooting too—some of the funniest lines come from that process. But generally Fran and I tend to do dialogue, side by side, staring at the computer. She's either on the floor writing and I'm typing, or sometimes she's typing and I'll sit down next to her and put my feet up on the desk and watch her type, because she hates that!" Philippa laughs. "Sometimes she's had a pass at a scene or I've had a pass at a scene and then we work it up together."

Fran and Philippa tended to write from contemporary perspectives, determined that the film should work for a modern audience. Peter, while not feeling dutybound to follow the original film exactly, served as its guardian. "We have to find stuff in it that we connect to and find interesting ourselves, Fran and I," says Philippa, "and there'd be moments where Pete would say this isn't *King Kong* anymore. And it's like, 'Well, you're right, it's not.' And we'd go back."

Although the heart of the story lies with Kong and Ann, much of the dramatic tension in the storytelling derives from the character of Carl Denham. Denham drives the story forward, initiating the journey to Skull Island and repeatedly pushing his friends further into danger, so an early concern for the writers was to figure out what could be driving this character.

"Often we'll work backwards," says Philippa, "and there's that key moment when Denham walks out onto that stage—Kong, the Eighth Wonder of the World—what's he feeling, what's he thinking? It's a moment of triumph for Denham. That told us that we needed for him to hear that he was a screwup in the beginning of the story. It's all about not being a failure."

And from there came the vision of how to kickstart the story: Philippa had a sudden image of Carl Denham running down the street with cans of film in his hands. "I remembered this wonderful story that I'd been told about Orson Welles being given money to shoot a western in Spain, and instead he shot *Chimes at Midnight*, which is [his] brilliant Falstaff film. He completely duped them and on the weekends he shot another movie. And I said that's the feel of this guy . . . he steals his own movie—which also had an element of Pete in it which I liked!"

Other aspects of Orson Welles's personality were folded into Carl Denham: "He's a passionate filmmaker, he's a risk-taker—you've got to love him, like you've got to love Orson Welles and his wild genius and his courage, but he was also someone who wasted a lot of his talent and was reckless with other people's lives. So in terms of the storytelling tension, he's a lovable, charming rogue who dupes his best friend. He's a force of nature, this little whirlwind who sucks people into his orbit through sheer force of personality. We want you to love him right up to the moment that you don't love him anymore because what he's doing is actually destructive."

It was the male romantic lead, the character of

Jack Driscoll, that underwent perhaps the biggest overhaul. In 1933, he was the first mate of the *Venture* and something of a "macho lunkhead," as Peter describes him. Adrien Brody's Jack Driscoll is a playwright, with touches of Arthur Miller and Eugene O'Neill in him, one of a new breed of writers revolutionizing American theater with social realism.

"It's much more interesting to us to have this New York born and bred intellectual playwright in the middle of a jungle than to have this seasoned adventurer/first mate of the ship go after Ann," says Philippa. "As soon as you set up that dynamic where you have this big macho guy wearing his heroics on his sleeve, it becomes a pissing contest between two men. It's not about her anymore, it's about these two guys—and Kong's the biggest alpha male in the world, so it becomes no contest."

Defining and balancing the Kong/Ann/Jack triangle was not easy. "It's very hard to generate a successful love story with Ann and Jack whilst you're playing the emotional connection between Ann and Kong," says Peter. "You have this very poignant story—which is not a romance, it's a relationship between Kong and Ann—and the poignancy of this creature who opens up his heart to her, which is ultimately his undoing. And you have at the same time more of a traditional love story between Ann and Jack. It's hard to juggle."

"We didn't want the character of Jack to be going up against Kong," says Philippa. "We wanted him to be going up against how he feels. He is physically brave, but not emotionally brave until the end of the movie. And we like the idea that he's incongruous in that jungle setting, he doesn't know how to use a tommy gun. But then we also wanted someone who was terrified but does it anyway, because that's true

*Jack Black as Carl Denham.*

14

Adrien Brody as Jack Driscoll.

Kyle Chandler as Bruce Baxter.

courage. And yet he still can't say what she needs to hear the way that Kong can. He needs to say, 'I came because I love you.'"

The original character of Jack Driscoll, as portrayed in 1933 by Bruce Cabot, does put in an appearance of sorts in the 2005 version of *King Kong*. Bruce Baxter, played by Kyle Chandler, is an actor who is starring as the first mate in Denham's adventure movie. The dialogue for a scene played by Ann Darrow and Bruce Baxter was lifted straight from a scene between Ann and first mate Jack Driscoll in the 1933 film.

As *Kong* fans know, Ann Darrow was played in the original *King Kong* by Fay Wray. Peter, Fran, and Philippa were fortunate enough to meet Fay Wray not long before she died in 2004. Her Ann was very much the thirties ideal of a vulnerable, beautiful young girl. "Every man's fantasy," says Philippa, laughing. "But I think women wanted it to be like that too. . . . Women were driving a lot of that sentiment, as they do now. Women needed to feel vulnerable, and they wanted to be beautiful, and they wanted that amazing sense of being able to disarm a man with their beauty. Believe me, I saw Fay at age ninety-six sit there and look at Peter when he said could he take a picture. She smiled at him, and I thought this woman must have been lethal when she was younger, because she was still beautiful, still charming, still could tell that Peter was completely smitten."

Fay Wray's Ann did not respond to Kong as does Naomi's Ann. "In the 1933 version, it really was about the beast being in love with beauty," says Philippa. "It wasn't a mutual thing, she was terrified. It was a monster. Fran and I had a lot of talks about that—the monster from the id and what was it, what did he represent? Whatever steps out of that jungle is our greatest fear. But he's not."

Ann's newly conceived vaudeville background

gave the writers an opportunity to toughen her up. To flesh out that background, they read books by Gypsy Rose Lee's sister June Havoc, once a famous vaudevillian. "That's why Jack Driscoll's play is called *Cry Havoc*," says Philippa. "June Havoc wrote an amazing biography of the times, called *Early Havoc*. Fran fell in love with that stuff, and I can see why. It just gave Ann some spirit and spunk. She's a tough little cookie. But she's also vulnerable. She's had a hard life. As Manny says, 'Life ain't been easy for you, kid.'"

So, when Kong takes Ann to his killing ground, she is armed with her hard-knocks vaudeville training. She fights for her life with a comedy routine, and although he is a tough audience, Kong responds to her performance. It is the first step in a series of communications that takes the relationship far beyond that of monster and terrified captive.

Kong is being created as a digital creature, but Peter asked Andy Serkis to play a role in shaping Kong's performance. Andy was the actor behind the groundbreaking performance of Gollum, a fully digital character in *The Lord of the Rings* films. "With someone like Andy," says Philippa, "you know that Kong is never just going to be a monster. There's got to be a complex character relationship."

Gorillas are social creatures, so it is not implausible that he connects on some level with Ann. "Kong is completely open with his feelings. He's just who he is and unafraid emotionally. There's this incredible sense of loyalty, because once he decides you're family, then you're part of the group, which is what he does with Ann."

Philippa sees aspects of Quasimodo in Kong. The moment when he recognizes himself in one of Skull Island's ancient statues parallels Quasimodo's recognition of his own hideousness when he looks at some gargoyles.

"Fran remembered seeing *The Hunchback of*

*Notre Dame* when she was younger, so we got it out and we were watching the crowds chasing Quasimodo through the streets, and she said, 'New York has to turn on him.' For me, it was [the idea of] sanctuary that resonated as I watched it.

"Kong goes to the top of the Empire State Building. Why does he do that? Because it is sanctuary. But there is no sanctuary up there, because we live in a modern age and there are things like airplanes, and they can get him. He doesn't know that, he took her to the safest place he could see, and to him, rising up above the jungle below is the most natural thing—he's always done that."

Questioning, always questioning, adding shades of complexity to the characters and story: writing the script is a seemingly never-ending process for Peter, Fran, and Philippa. As filming progresses, as the actors breathe life into the characters, the storytelling and dialogue continue to evolve, with scenes being rewritten almost right up to the moment they go be-

fore the cameras. Even during postproduction, lines can be rerecorded in the sound studio and the actors can be called back to film changed or new scenes. "That's the way Pete likes to work," says Philippa. "He never shuts doors on things. He likes to be able to feel the pace and the tension, and how things are playing and working, and what's successful and what's not successful."

Despite developing the characters and redefining the way that they operate within the story, the writers have kept close to the structure of the 1933 film: a first act in New York, the journey to hell on Skull Island, and a return to New York for the tragic final act. "That's pretty much exactly like the original film," says Peter. "We didn't want to do anything radically different like suddenly having Kong survive at the end of the film, because it worked really great first time round. It's a wonderful movie, the original, it's a great story. If we can get close to capturing that, then we'll be very happy."

19

An early exterior design concept of Kong's lair by Gus Hunter.

Even as Peter Jackson, Fran Walsh, and Philippa Boyens raced to complete *The Return of the King* and get their early ideas for the *King Kong* script down on paper, concept illustrations started pouring out.

"We didn't have much of a brief at that stage," says conceptual designer Gus Hunter. "I would do artwork and it would be sent in a package to Peter, and he would have a look at it over the weekend. I think at that time we were taking bits and pieces of the 1996 *King Kong* script—knowing that it would be changed, but it was a place to start. Now and again we would get dribs and drabs of feedback through Richard Taylor, and he'd say, 'Pete's quite happy, do some more.' So I'd carry on, just immerse myself and have fun."

A key conceptual design focus was formulating the look of Skull Island: "What does the jungle look like? I was really blown away by the original when I was a young chap, and I got the movie out again and watched it a few times," says Gus. "The real task was trying to re-create the Skull Island of the original movie, but have Peter's feel to it."

Peter loves the stylized look of the 1933 movie. It harkens back to the fantastic biblical and literary illustrations of Gustave Doré, a nineteenth-century French illustrator whose work inspires artists and filmmakers to this day.

# CREATING SKULL ISLAND

"Gustave Doré," explains Richard Taylor, "had a particular style where he lit environments with an immensely strong central light on the central figure, whether that be Moses or Christ or whoever, and then allowed the outside of the frame to drop away to a very dark tone, creating visually stunning and filmic images a long time before film was ever invented. The technique that Willis O'Brien and Marcel Delgado used to do the special effects for the original *King Kong* complemented this sort of artwork, and it made for very beautiful filmmaking, on a par with movies made today."

The special effects scenes in the 1933 *King Kong* were filmed using a layering technique. A typical jungle shot might have live or miniature foliage in the foreground, several clear sheets of plate glass framed with painted vines and foliage in the middle ground, more three-dimensional foliage between each sheet of glass, and a matte painting or previously filmed stop-animation footage back-projected onto a large translucent screen in the background. The dark foregrounds, midtoned middle grounds, and bright, pale backgrounds created an illusion of great depth and distance, with the actors highlighted in the midground.

"There was a certain look to the original film where you went from dark to light

An older study by Jeremy Bennett of the Brontosaurs.

Above: Early design concept by Gus Hunter showing Skull Island's tortured coastline and broken landscape as seen from a distance.
Below: A painting by Jeremy Bennett, taking a previz frame and extrapolating on it to create a creepy feeling for the swamp.

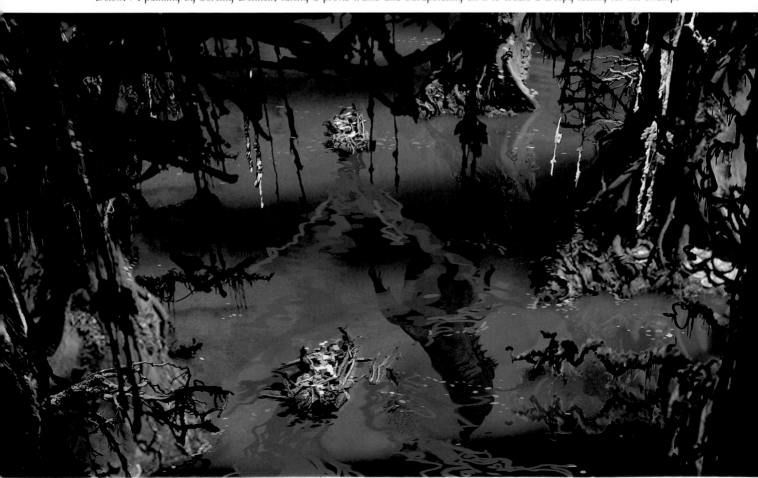

Below: One of a series of studies by Jeremy Bennett of the Brontosaur stampede environment.

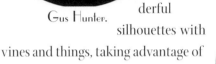

Gus Hunter.

to dark to light," says conceptual designer Jeremy Bennett. "There was a nice tunnel-like effect with the old glass matte paintings— these wonderful silhouettes with vines and things, taking advantage of the smoky, brighter backgrounds."

"In a way it's quite simple, how they did it in those days," says Gus.

"It's very simple, but I've actually found it surprisingly difficult to replicate," says Jeremy, laughing.

Once preproduction for *King Kong* was in full swing, Gus and Jeremy produced conceptual paintings at an average of four each per day. Sometimes it

Jeremy Bennett.

ultimately took as many as seventy paintings to capture the essence of a single Skull Island environment. They were joined for a time by Alan Lee, preproduction conceptual artist, at the tail end of his involvement on *The Lord of the Rings*. Alan produced many beautiful concept drawings for Skull Island, and his ideas for the village had a direct influence on the layout of this huge set piece. Gus and Jeremy worked independently of each other and met with Peter twice a week.

"Peter always said, 'I'd prefer if you guys actually didn't look at each other's work,'" says Jeremy. "So come Friday, I had no idea what Gus had done, and he had no idea what I had done, or how many we'd each done. We'd be pinning them up, looking over our shoulders at the other guy's work—so nerve-racking, because you just wanted to crack a design for something."

An environment study by Jeremy Bennett illustrating the journey from the coast to the village.

*Arrival at Cairo of Prisoners of Minich* by Gustave Doré.

"But it was good," says Gus, "because there were two different styles. . . . [Peter] would choose bits and pieces of both our artwork and he would tell us to do a second pass at it. And we'd meet back after three days. We'd refine it until we had it. Sometimes we'd be lucky and hit it straight off, but that was very rare."

Left: An early study of the wall by Jeremy Bennett. "I imagined the gate totally blocked with debris: tree trunks, rocks, anything they could set their hands on," says Jeremy. Right: An early study of the New York docks by Jeremy Bennett.

"Peter's incredibly positive," says Jeremy. "He's very good at telling you what he likes and why. It's very rare that you come away feeling brutally critiqued. But you just want him to like it so they can move ahead and start building things, because everyone's waiting on you.

"In some areas he would have a really clear idea. He would even draw something on the whiteboard. Other times he'd just say, 'Come back in a couple of days and show me what you've got.' . . . Pete knows exactly what he's after. He won't sign off until he gets it. You might show him a painting that he'll really like, and he might not change anything about the idea, but the composition—the placement of stuff—he might have a few notes on, and he's always right. . . . And in that sense I really enjoy working with him because his aesthetic is so refined."

The ancient architecture of Skull Island presented a special challenge to the conceptual designers: "It couldn't be any architecture that anyone has seen before," says Gus. "We had to do a lot of concepts of what the wall was going to look like. Pete didn't want the ancient-civilization architecture to be too sophisticated."

"It wasn't like the Aztecs or the Mayans at the height of their civilization, for example," says Jeremy. "Not as advanced. If you look at the structure of the wall and what it was built from, it's monumental in its size but it doesn't have the finish of dressed stone by the Egyptians. You can put a credit card through the cracks of the blocks—it's not an Incan masterpiece."

New York, being an existing city, did not require much in the way of conceptual design. "We did a bit of painting on the look of the dock area," says Jeremy. "We've always got a dark shape—whether it's ropes or a bit of a crane or crates—in the foreground, so we've managed to find ways of duplicating the basic composition from the original here as well."

Over at Stone Street Studios, the art department's concept room is wallpapered with Jeremy's and Gus's paintings. In Weta Workshop's miniatures studio, where sculptors are carving Skull Island landscapes, concept paintings are skewered to blocks of polystyrene and scattered over workbenches. The concept designs form the basis for the construction of live-action jungle sets, miniatures, and digital

123/001

Conceptual art: Brontosaurus grazing environment..

Conceptual art by Gus Hunter illustrating an ancient overgrown city within the Island,
which has become a lush grazing area for the Brontosaurs.
Inset: Previz shot of Brontosaur environment. The previz was done before the concept art.

backdrops and give everyone a clear sense of the look and mood Peter wants for each setting.

In the final weeks of principal photography, Jeremy and Gus are still hard at it. "We're now fully immersed in the visual effects, which is all the blue-screen stuff," says Gus. "We're designing the matte paintings for the matte painters."

"Which is good fun," adds Jeremy, "because we're almost having a second pass at those environ-ments now—you can clean them up or refine them, and anything you might have missed, or an aesthetic that may have evolved a little bit, you can now advance."

"Watching the shots now coming together, they are starting to look so beautiful and so evocative and so filmic," says Richard Taylor. "For me, Peter has found a wonderful balance between the very fantastical and a very gritty, very harsh, very real world."

Conceptual art by Gus Hunter giving the overall exterior look of Kong's lair.

Two key decisions defined the task that lay ahead for the makers of *King Kong*: one was to give the jungle a fantastical appearance; the other was to make 1933 New York look absolutely authentic. Those seemingly disparate decisions lead to the same conclusion: virtually every setting in the movie would need to be built from scratch.

"Everything shot on this movie, bar one or two minor instances, has been studio-based," says *King Kong* production designer Grant Major. "There are no locations, other than the Opera House and Civic Theater. Everything has been manufactured, be that set-wise or miniature-wise or done in the digital realm."

"At the outset, Peter had a couple of really interesting framing ideas," says Alex Funke, director of visual effects photography. "He said, 'I'm not updating the *King Kong* story. I'm keeping it in 1933. What I want to do is see what would happen if Willis O'Brien, the guy who did this stuff in 1933, had at that time the gadgets that we have today.' And he also said, 'I'd like people to say, "I knew New Zealand had some fantastic locations, but, wow, where did you find Skull Island?"'"

Shooting the Skull Island scenes on location in a real jungle might seem more practical than fabricating an extensive jungle in a studio. "We certainly thought about that idea at the beginning," admits director Peter Jackson. "But the 1933 jungles are very stylized, very much based on Gustave Doré's artwork. Things closest to you are silhouetted and dark, and as they go further away they get progressively flatter and brighter and foggier. I just couldn't imagine doing *King Kong* without somehow doing that, and it would be impossible to do it on location. You couldn't control the elements. That look is artificial, there's a certain art-directed style to it, and it has to be done in a very technically controllable way."

The stylized jungle in the 1933 *King Kong* was done with model trees, a series of glass paintings, and back projections. The jungle in the 2005 *King Kong* is a combination of live-action sets, miniatures, and digital elements. "We're doing a much more high-tech but ultimately similar style of layering," says Peter, "so we have very dark foregrounds and we're filming the actors in a piece of jungle with a lot of blue screen and green screen behind them, and then we'll have miniatures to create the ongoing depth of the jungle, and they'll be lit very much in the same way as the 1933 film.

"I want our Skull Island to feel like it's the same Skull Island that they used in 1933. I want people to feel like we'd traveled there and shot in the same places they

# FABRICATING REALITY

32

An interior Skull Island jungle set.

did. We're using different technical processes, but we're hopefully going to end up at the same place."

Manufacturing a jungle presents challenges, but Grant Major sees those challenges as being more manageable than shooting on location. "On *The Lord of the Rings* we were helicoptering crews to mountaintops," he says. "Building a piece of set in the studio is so much easier, with so much more potential to have exactly what we want, rather than *sort of* what we want. The challenge is to make all this man-made stuff feel real. . . . You've got to believe in this scratchy, prickly, dangerous environment."

Making the jungle believable turns out to involve lots of wind. Peter envisioned Skull Island as a windy environment, and that decision has had repercussions right down the line, for the miniatures, the digital environments, the sound department, and for the actors and crew on set.

"Wind has been with us since the beginning of

the shoot," says Peter. "Doing a jungle in a studio is a risky thing to do. So often you see movies where they look phony. So we've had big wind machines in the studio blowing the trees around. And then of course it's vital that the miniatures match. A miniature jungle looks like a model if you're not careful, but as soon as you start it moving and waving, it comes alive."

"Peter said, 'The thing I've never liked about miniatures of trees and woods is that they don't move. They're static. That kills the illusion. I want you to put wind on the trees,'" remembers miniatures maestro Alex Funke. "Well, you can see why nobody else has ever tried to do this. It's extremely hard! There's a huge amount of voodoo involved in the kind of wind, the kind of trees, how you articulate them, how you shoot them, how you light them. But the fact is that it does make a difference."

"I know the guys all tear their hair out, but it is

The New York City set in Wellington.

Digitally extending the set does not just mean adding upper floors to the topless building facades constructed for the back-lot set. The visual effects team has built a detailed three-dimensional digital model of the entire city. Senior visual effects supervisor Joe Letteri reckons that painstaking adherence to historical records has made it easier to build this digital version: "If you have a blueprint that you can follow, people aren't guessing how all the pieces have to fit together. But more importantly, we wanted to make sure that we were capturing the feel of 1930s New York because that time and era are really important to the feel of the story."

The drive for authenticity extends to every detail—the colors, the cars, the costumes. Everything was meticulously researched, right down to the numbers of people on the streets and the signs on the billboards in Times Square. "The movies that are playing in Times Square are all 1933 films, real films," says Peter. "It's Christmas, so we looked in 1933 newspapers and found out what films would have been playing in Times Square in December 1933, and those were the films that we put up on the adverts in the cinemas."

Peter wants the city portrayed in *King Kong* to be nothing less than the most authentic-looking Depression-era New York ever seen on film, and he is confident that it will be a convincing representation of the real New York. "People will think that we've shot there. There won't be anything giving away the fact that it's not actually New York, other than the fact that there are hundreds of old cars, and they'll wonder how we did it."

For Peter, it is all about transporting audiences to another place and time, and making sure that while they're there, it is a place and time they can believe in. "You just anchor the film in a real place," he says, "make everything as believable as possible."

worth it," says Peter "It'll look good. The wind is our friend."

Similar volumes of effort and determination have gone into creating a realistic Depression-era New York City. The art department and Weta Digital have been sticklers for historical accuracy, going to great lengths to track down images and archival records that would give them detailed blueprints for rebuilding a 1930s version of the city.

"Peter's always wanted realism," says Grant, who designed a huge New York set to be built on a studio back lot in Wellington. "We were never going to [film in] New York because it's not like Depression-era New York anymore, so it wasn't going to give us what we wanted. But back lots tend to close off the streets a lot, which is not really like New York either. New York's got scale to it. It's got these long vistas . . . and of course it's got the height. So our back-lot set was always going to be digitally extended."

Frames from the previz of the Empire State Building attack.

On Richard Frances-Moore's computer screen there is a rough animation of Kong in shades of gray. All around him are the shapes of Times Square—vehicles, theaters, people. Kong whirls around, confused and disoriented. He knocks over a car, his frustration building. The animation lacks color, sound, and any kind of detail, but the dynamics of the action tell the story: a desperate Kong is embarking on a destructive rampage through the streets of New York.

Richard is a lead animator at Weta Digital. The scene on his screen is a previsualization animatic, more commonly referred to as previz.

"Previz," explains Richard, "is using computer animation to do the storyboarding—the visual development of the film, shot by shot, before anything gets shot on set. It's a tool for Peter to be able to say, 'This is what I want the scene to look like.' It's an extension of storyboarding. For Kong we haven't done any [traditional] storyboarding at all."

Previsualization director Christian Rivers used to be a storyboard artist, most recently on *The Lord of the Rings*. "Peter would describe the shots for the film and I'd sketch them," he says. "Now we have a team of people, and rather than storyboard it, we discuss the scenes and the action and we animate in 3D—fairly roughly, but accurate to the broad strokes of what Peter wants."

The first scenes the previz team tackled were for the film's final sequence at the Empire State Building. "The script was still loose," says Richard, "but they knew they had to have Kong and the Empire State Building, so that's where we started."

"I think the Empire State Building sequence really brought a lot of people into what the film was going to be like," says lead animator Andrew Calder. "Initially when you come and work on *King Kong*, you think, 'Big adventure movie, silly monsters'—whereas the Empire State Building sequence has quite an impact. It's serious and tragic, and a lot of people really responded to it, even in previz form. It really sets the tone: 'Oh, *this* is the film we're working on.'"

Armed with conceptual artwork and a brief from Peter, the previz team starts each scene by developing choreography for the action. Kong's battle with the V-Rexes has evolved into a nine-minute sequence, but in the script it was just a few words long: "It was 'Kong fights three V-Rexes. *Rarrr!* Battle ensues,'" says Christian, laughing. "There was no time limit on it. Peter said, 'You've got three V-Rexes, you've got Kong, you've got Ann, you've got a jungle, come up with some ideas.' So we spent a bit of time just giving him some crazy options. He picked ideas that he liked, and they ran through his filter and then came back out in the sequence order that they now stand in the film."

PREVIZ

For many scenes, the previz human characters were animated using motion capture, whereby a live actor's movements are captured on computer. Long before the start of principal photography and the arrival of the actors on set, Christian, Peter Jackson, production assistant Mike Wallis, and animation director Eric Leighton performed most of the human characters on the motion-capture stage.

"We started using motion capture to quickly get humans that we could throw into the scene and interact with our big beasties," says Eric Leighton. "So we all dressed up in Velcro and spandex mocap suits with little dots all over ourselves, and we performed all of the roles. I did a lot of Jimmy and Hayes, Christian did a lot of Adrien's stuff, Pete did lots of Denham, and we all danced around and threw ourselves on the ground and hit invisible bugs."

The beauty of 3D animation is that, once the previz artists have roughed out a sequence of action, it can be viewed from any direction as if through virtual cameras. In that respect, it is just like live action: one can choreograph the action and then set up cameras to film it from particular angles.

"We would animate the previz just looking through one particular virtual camera, like standing back wide and watching it all happen," says Christian. "And then Pete says, 'Okay, yeah, I like what they're doing there, now give me a camera where we start in low, a close-up on the rex, and swing the camera around while Kong sweeps through frame.' So then you follow certain actions as if you were a cameraman, and it gives the whole sequence a really natural dynamic that sometimes isn't there in visual effects shots because they're composed and so meticulously engineered."

Once the previz artists have generated the raw footage—the close-ups, the wide shots, the low angles—it is all handed over to Peter and editor Jamie Selkirk, who do a final selection of shots and then edit the footage together, essentially providing a rough cut of the scene before the cameras even start rolling.

Previz is the roughest of animations, and yet it communicates a surprising amount of information. Peter has used it every day on set to show the crew and the actors what he has in mind for each scene. It can also be played back on a "video assist" monitor with the live action superimposed, so that Peter can make sure that the actors are appropriately positioned in relation to the computer-generated elements in each shot.

The previz cut of each sequence will also be used as "a tool for planning the visual effects, and by every other department," says visual effects supervisor Ben

Left: Previz of the Brontosaur stampede. Information is burnt into each frame: 866 is the frame number; (24 - 981) is the frame range for the sequence; Lens: 28mm is virtual camera information which is important for the camera units; 123 is the scene number; 043 is the shot number. The sbs number is an internal previz number. Right: Previz shot for Kong's fight against the V-Rexes.

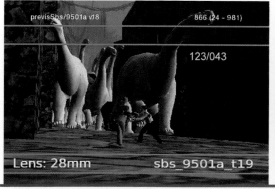

Skull Island - Kong Capture at Wall - 163/017

Top left inset shot is the previz image, which was created first. Below it is Jeremy Bennett's concept art for Kong's capture. Here we see Kong leaping in pursuit of Ann and Jack. This study was done for the miniatures and digital departments.

Snow. "The art department will use this information to help create the sets. If the second unit is shooting some material, then Peter will use these to explain to the second unit director the sorts of elements that he wants. And the previz helps Miniatures and Workshop plan what sort of models to build and how they should be shot."

"We build a whole 3D environment for the previz," explains Christian. "For instance, we'll design a terrain for where Kong is fighting, and Weta Workshop will build pretty much the terrain to match that."

At a later stage of production, the previz team goes into a kind of postviz phase, combining live-action footage with tidied-up previz, to give the digital and miniatures teams more specific and up-to-date information they can use in finishing the effects shots.

As the previz artists animate their way at breakneck speed through the movie, they are very much at the hub of the production, helping Peter to tell the story of *King Kong*. "All the people who do previz have to have a good sense of storytelling and how to move a camera to tell a story," says Richard. "It's a jack-of-all-trades, master of none."

Top: Macy's building in Herald Square, dressed with Christmas decorations. Left: Construction phase of the Burlesque Theater. Right: The Burlesque Theater is redressed as the Princess Theater for a later scene. Opposite page: Burlesque Theater architectural plan (blueprint).

Rather than find filming locations and turn back time in present-day New York, the *King Kong* production team decided to re-create several blocks of thirties-era New York on a vacant site in Seaview, an industrial suburb just a twenty-minute drive from downtown Wellington.

Wellington is a hilly city, with a reputation for winds that occasionally howl up to gale force, and finding a flat, sheltered site large enough for New York proved to be impossible. The Seaview site is flat, at least, but is surrounded by fuel-storage tanks and exposed to the cold winds that whip across Wellington's harbor.

"Believe me, we looked all over Wellington not to choose that space, because we knew how exposed it was," says producer and first assistant director Carolynne Cunningham. "But there

was nothing that was flat enough, big enough, and had the facilities around it to be able to put in all the trucks and the unit people and everything that's required. So we got stuck out there in the middle of the fuel tanks, with emergency procedures in place in case something went boom.

"It was such a big set and the art department worked like Trojans to get it done," she says. "They had rain, they had wind, they had everything that could possibly slow them down."

The script required settings for Times Square, Herald Square, a low-rent district, and a variety of streets in different parts of the city. Fortunately, Times Square and Herald Square have similar layouts with Broadway cutting diagonally through each, so a plan was hatched to build Times Square with

## NEW YORK, WELLINGTON

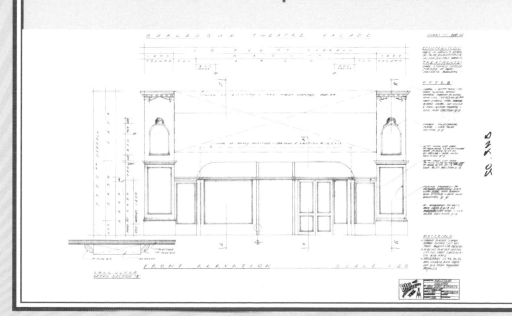

part of Broadway, Seventh Avenue, and several cross streets, then transform it midshoot to Herald Square on Sixth Avenue. Running parallel to the avenue was a road lined with typical tenement buildings, dubbed Tenement Street. It catered to the very opening sequence of the film, a scene-setting series of vignettes of life in 1930s New York.

"New York was big. New York takes the cake in terms of big sets," says Dan Hennah, supervising art director. "The site was just big enough to accommodate it. The expectation was winds in excess of one hundred kilometers an hour, so we used our good old reliable container technology."

"Container technology" is the ingenious use of walls of shipping containers to anchor building facades so they won't topple or fly away in a gale. The huge green or blue screens, used where the background will need to be replaced by a digital environment or backdrop, can also be supported by walls of containers. The short streets and avenues of the New York set dead-end in green screens.

"You can hire a container for two bucks a day," says construction supervisor Ed Mulholland. "So it's a cheap, very strong option for putting up the screens, rather than doing a big scaffolding work. It's all engineer-approved. If you look behind the set of New York, you'll see we've put a lot of containers down, put twenty ton of water barrels in them to counterweight them, and then tied the back of the set off to the containers—basically using the containers as a huge weight to hold the set together."

Accordingly, the theaters, shops, and tenement buildings lining the streets of New York are just one story high. "Our sets are all two containers high, which is five meters," says production designer Grant Major, "so there was a five-meter limit to all the sets we built—which happily is pretty much where the street level stuff and the tops of the canopies finished. And then everything above that will be digitally added in. That's a job I'm doing for Weta Digital at the moment—going round all the sets that we built and identifying the building type and textures and signs that will go on all those extended pieces."

Once Weta Digital's visual effects wizards have worked their magic, New York's skyscrapers will look tall and the avenues long, but the streets and buildings around the two squares may look a little skinnier than usual. "We scaled our New York sets down by about twenty percent," Grant says. "We just didn't have the space and the budget to build it full scale, but through a camera lens I don't think you'd ever know."

Other than the reduction in scale, extraordinary efforts were made to match the look of 1930s New York. To that end, a team of researchers sought out every accessible photographic record of the period to serve as a design guide.

"It's been almost two years of extensive research," says researcher Sarah Milnes. "New York was so different from what it is now. We concentrated mainly on the buildings to start off with, just getting a general look, but then it goes down to small details like

Mid-construction/painting phase on a corner of Times Square.

what was the window frame made out of, or what color was the original. All the photos are in black and white so it was quite hard to tell what colors things were.

"We found a lot of stuff on the Internet, accessing the New York Public Library online and e-mailing or phoning research librarians over there—or an expert in shipping or theatrical productions. And if you get the information from one source, you've got to back it up from somewhere else."

The research team also ferreted out photographs and information about the inhabitants of New York and the day-to-day details of their lives. "We looked at how people were living," says Sarah, "how much things cost, what sort of work people were doing, the food that they would eat, their general lifestyle and living conditions, the soup lines, the protests, what sort of things they would protest about, what signs they would have; also the ethnic makeup of New York, what socioeconomic groups would be in certain areas, and then things like costumes—small bits and pieces on every aspect."

After studying New York for two years, Sarah went out to the set during filming. "It makes your hair stand on end," she says. "It's a little bit creepy because it's so real. You take photos on set and convert them to black and white, and they look exactly like some of those original pictures."

The walls of Grant Major's office in the art department at Stone Street Studios are papered with floor plans, color charts, and photographs of New York, including one of Times Square. A movie sign in a photograph pinpoints the date it was taken as April 1933. "It's one of our prime reference photographs," he says. "It has many of the shops that we copied. We also did a people count of that photograph to judge how many extras we'd need on any given day. Per block, I think there were one hundred and fifty-five people in that shot. And we counted vehicles on the street.

"We copied a lot of the signage. We wanted to get it exactly right. When you look at any of the photographs, it's a sea of signage—not just advertising material, but a lot of civic stuff, right down to park-

Peter Jackson walks the streets of New York City.

Kalamazoo Diner in downtown New York City.

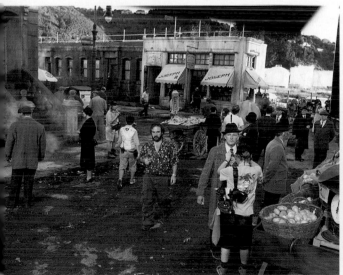

ing signs and street signage—a huge amount of detail. We had six graphic artists working for months and months on all that, and a similar number of sign writers. And then we had quite a few electric signs—on the theater canopies in Times Square in particular."

Grant is adamant that faithfully re-creating the finest details of period photographs is worth the effort. "The more you look into these photographs, the more fantastic detail there is," he says. "Truth is stranger than fiction in some ways, and the truth of these photographs is far more interesting than what you can conjure up in your mind as a fantasy version of it. . . . And also we want to make Americans, particularly New Yorkers, feel comfortable with the whole thing. There'd be nothing worse than them getting into this movie and then not believing their New York. Gritty realism is what I was after—in all its casualness and its busyness."

The gritty reality of the New York set was that it took hundreds of people months to build it. "We threw people at it," says Dan Hennah. "We had the site for six months, so we had a bit of time, but when we were busy trying to get other sets ready, we kept stealing people off New York and pushing them into other sets, so it was a bit of a push to get New York ready at the end. But it was always going to be, to get the degree of detail and authenticity that we felt it warranted."

The roads were laid early on in the building schedule so that, over time, they would be weathered by sun and rain, and the dirt tracked over them by construction vehicles. "Peter was very keen on the gritty, textural look to everything," says Grant. "All the period photos of the times show a lot of litter on the streets, and the streets didn't have the money spent on them so they were starting to degrade. So that suited us, from that gritty point of view and also from the

Barber shop and hardware store on New York City street.

budget point of view. There was a delicate balance between the money we had to spend and the look we were after and the period fidelity we wanted."

"We poured all our own curbing and pavements, and all our own cobblestones," says Dan, "but we had roading contractors lay the major tar seal for the rest of the streets. . . . And then we added a huge amount of old newspapers and cabbage leaves and dry autumn leaves."

Railway contractors installed the rails for the tram. "That was something we didn't want to take any risks with," says Dan. "We had a real tram, but we didn't have the resources to put in an electric rail, so we put in a piece of steel channel with a chain in it, and we put a winch on the tram so that it winched itself up and down the chain. The chain didn't move, but the tram did. It was a background

thing to a large degree, but it was a great element to have, because it's such a big-scale piece that even peripherally it helps with the illusion that you are in New York."

The job of pumping steam out of manholes on the streets fell to the special effects team, who laid nearly two kilometers of piping under the roads. "We had a couple of big boilers and each outlet was individually controlled," says special effects coordinator Steve Ingram, "so if one outlet was where they wanted the camera, it could be turned right down, or you could pump more steam out of the ones in deep background."

Getting the underground pipes laid out for the steam system turned into a nightmare job. The site is at sea level, so the team immediately ran up against the water table. As fast as they dug plumbing

43

The special effects team makes artificial snow.

44

Burlesque Theater lit and ready for shooting a night scene.

trenches, the holes filled up with water. To add to the problem, there was constant rain.

"There was so much water that the steam pipes wouldn't get up to temperature," Steve explains, "because they were being cooled by the water they were sitting in. We had to dig those bits up again and encase them in concrete so the water couldn't get to them. It was a huge job, but we got it. We had seventy-odd steam sources plumbed in there, all individually controlled, and it worked really well."

Steve's team also trimmed the streets with piles of snow. "Peter's idea was that when it had snowed, it was dirty," Steve says. "It had been cleaned out of someone's doorway and thrown into piles with the rubbish and dirt, and it didn't make the city look beautiful."

Five thousand sacks of bark mulch—ground-up bark—were used to bulk and shape the snow piles. Each heap of bark was covered with a layer of Dacron, and insulation foam was sprayed over the Dacron, forming a hard crust. Around the edges the special effects team sprinkled Epsom salts, which glistened under the lighting.

Stairs to nowhere and ten steel support pillars were all that was built of the station and elevated

A wide shot of Times Square. A lighting tower is affixed on the top of the set for night shoots. The hills in the background will be replaced with digital New York City images.

track for the el system. The topless pillars, standing in pairs, marked the route of the absent train track. "It started off snaking from Broadway, then we took it away altogether for some shots, and then we brought it back in and ran it all the way down the avenue as part of the Herald Square setup," says Dan Hennah. "It took three men twenty minutes to move one of those pillars."

Eight engineers worked full-time for months building lampposts, street signs, and wrought-iron fences. A team of sculptors carved the decorative moldings for every building facade out of polystyrene. Set finishers textured, painted, and dirtied-down exterior surfaces and painted marblelike flooring in entranceways. Props buyers and props makers supplied merchandise for every shop, and set dressers arranged them in the windows.

"I had twenty-odd people there," says supervising set dresser Tanea Chapman. "We gave each dresser eight shops to take care of, so for us it was an opportunity to have a little bit of creative freedom. . . . Grant walked round with me and said roughly what he wanted: 'This is a shoe shop, it'll have a stand of shoes. This will be a restaurant.' The great thing about having so many people doing shops side by side [is that] it did look quite gen-

46

The Lyric Vaudeville Theater where Ann performs, dressed and ready for shooting.

uinely like different people had done their own window display, which is what window dressing is all about."

At times the art department swelled to almost the man power required for *The Lord of the Rings*. "When we were majorly stretched with New York, we had 475 to 500 people in the art department," says art department manager Chris Hennah. "New York was one of those sets that seemed like it was simple, but really was quite tricky. We had a far bigger set-dressing department than we had on *The Lord of the Rings* because there were so many shops and all the stuff in the shops had to be purchased.

"You'd go out there and it was just bustling with people," she recalls. "There was a lot of stress, because we had a very tight time frame, but there was a really good spirit. Everybody was helping each other, working with each other—[it was] pretty cool to be a part of."

The switch from Times Square, the showbiz part of town, to Herald Square, a department-store area, happened over a weekend, but some parts of the set were transformed overnight. "We built sets in front of other sets so that we could take them away halfway through shooting to reveal the sets underneath," says Grant. "And we had various prefabri-

The Lyric Vaudeville Theater redressed as the Capitol Theater for a later scene.

cated additions that we could put on to change things as well."

The Alhambra Theater had its canopy craned off to turn it into the Marbridge Building. The automat café in Times Square was a clipped-on facade with Macy's shop frontage behind it, preset with Christmas-themed window displays. The facades could be removed overnight, and a quick switch of canopies completed the transformation.

Many shops just had a change of signs and window dressing to convert them from, say, a drapery to a menswear shop. Some buildings had a quick re-paint and elements such as the door repositioned.

One restaurant was simply boarded over. "It was on a corner that, as it transpired, we saw more of than we expected to," says Dan. "So we turned it into a derelict shop that had been boarded up. It happened a lot in those times. That was always our fallback: if it doesn't work, board it up. But we only did it once!"

Peter and crew spent just three weeks filming on the New York set, mostly at night, along with five hundred extras who were hired to populate the city streets.

"The set was great and the extras were really cool," says Carolynne Cunningham, first assistant di-rector. "They were chosen really well, they were just

Peter Jackson gives direction during a night shoot.

good people. It's a thankless job and they were great-spirited and they did everything that was asked of them. It's pretty tough to be asked to go out there every night for a couple of weeks and do a lot of waiting around, and then do something for a little while, and then do a lot more waiting around. They were really good about it."

Filming is a notoriously slow process. In the drive to get everything just right, each shot takes an age to set up, and take after take to film. On *King Kong*, each shot was covered by three different cameras, which added to the setup time since the action, lighting, and background had to be just right from the point of view of all three cameras.

"Some of the shots are so big and complicated, you'd be mad not to cover it from as many angles as you can," says Carolynne. "It also gives Peter and Fran more choices in the cutting room."

The extras each played several different roles. One day they might be angry protesters, one night they might be fleeing from Kong in shock and terror.

Kong will, of course, be added later by the digital effects team at Weta Digital. "We didn't have a twenty-five-foot gorilla rampaging down the street," says Carolynne. "All his interaction, crashing into buildings, and things coming off and things being damaged, it's all going to be digital. All we could do was shoot the surrounding plates, which was the action that goes on around Kong while he's doing that. You can use previz as the tool to see where he's going to be, what he's going to do, and then shoot many people running around the streets in fear, and Jack in his car chasing him."

Adrien Brody, who plays Jack Driscoll, got to do some of his own stunt driving around the streets of the New York set. "I got to drive a thirties cab like a maniac through those streets, which was really, really exciting," says Adrien.

Adrien is an accomplished driver. His training ground for fast driving was the streets of real New York. He grew up there and spent much of his spare time fixing up muscle cars and drag racing. Even so, it is highly unusual for an actor to do his own stunt driving on a movie. Typically a stunt double would stand in for the actor to do such scenes.

"Pete took a gamble with me that day," says Adrien. "He basically mounted four cameras on the car and put me in it—and me driving away from Kong and essentially doing every stunt that I knew, which was reverse 180s and 360s and the e-brakes, slides, and then narrowly missing extras and cars and elevated train tracks, and jumping the curb. It was so exciting."

"He did it really well," says Carolynne. "He didn't do the really, really dangerous stuff—actually hitting the fruit stand and taking the corners very fast when there's stunt people and extras on the streets. That kind of thing we did with Tony Marsh, Adrien's stunt double."

Adrien thinks that the close-ups on Jack driving will look all the more convincing for having been done for real. "You can't fake it," he says. "You have the lights reflecting off the window and you have the vibration of the whole vehicle and the camera shaking and shuddering. And I was nervous, so it was exciting to use that nervous energy to really amp it up. If I had made a mistake, everybody would have gone home early because I had every camera on the car." He laughs. "That's probably one of the most fun days I've had on any movie. All those years of driving around New York paid off."

49

Cushman's Produce stand, where Ann steals an apple and meets Carl Denham.

It is December 1933 and the shop windows in the streets around Herald Square are dressed for Christmas. On display are countless goodies to entice shoppers: hats, cigars, shoes, beauty products, women's fashions, flags, toys, novelty gifts, and more—each and every item provided by the art department's props buyers, prop makers, and set dressers.

Phred Palmer, head props buyer, sees the buyers as the hunters and gatherers of the props department. For a time, four buyers were scouting for thirties-style goods to fill the shopwindows on the New York set. They searched Internet trading sites and went to every antique store and secondhand shop they knew. "It's physically impossible for [only] one person to do all that shopping."

Mercifully, much of the merchandise in the shops could be empty packaging. "We bought thousands of empty tins, and our graphic designers just went crazy and did these fantastic tin labels. We gave them the tin sizes, the box sizes, and the bottle sizes, and there was a whole minipackaging department, about four of them, just getting the graphics, the boxes, the bottles, and sticking the labels on. It was insane—weeks and weeks of spray gluing."

Days were spent photocopying specially designed magazine covers and gluing them onto old magazines to put on magazine stands. A Wellington newspaper, *The Dominion Post*, did a special print run of front and back pages for the New York dailies. "We had a designer who designed *The New York Post* and *The New York Times* and a variety of different newspapers, and then liaised with *The Dominion Post*, and they did the fronts and backs for us and filled it with their own paper," says set dresser Tanea Chapman. "So then we could have people sitting reading the paper, and if you did get a close-up, it was a completely authentic script and headlines."

Shops such as bakeries and butcheries needed to have fresh produce on display, but it was summertime in New Zealand when the shops were dressed. "You can't leave meat lying around in a film set in the hot sun of January and February," says prop maker Tony Drawbridge, "and obviously they can't keep on replacing it. So we made all these molds of it. We had someone pouring it up out of urethane foam, and then it would be painted and go and sit in the butcher's shop."

The prop makers replicated chickens, sides of beef, mince, sausages, liver, and whole muttons—all made from molds of real meat. But first they had to make the molds—a messy and, on one occasion, maggoty job.

"The mold-making process takes time," says prop maker Jake Yocum. "I was

# THE LIE FACTORY

molding a sheep and it mustn't have been too fresh because the maggots appeared pretty damn quick. You could smell it, it was pretty nasty. When you're casting dead flesh, there's a bad smell to it if you leave it. It gets kind of cooked in the fiberglass and silicone."

The cars on New York's streets were also the responsibility of the props department. Props master Nick Weir made up a wish list and put out a call for vintage vehicles. Twenty-five fully operational vintage cars in pristine condition were provided and driven during filming by their owners, who were only too pleased to see their cars in such an authentic thirties setting, as if transported back through time to their heyday.

But the props team also needed vehicles they could convert into taxis, delivery vans, military and police vehicles, plus stunt vehicles that could be crunched or crashed. Rather than deface some lovingly maintained vintage vehicles, they sleuthed out and bought some sadder-looking models, the kind you find smothered under dust and cobwebs in old farm sheds.

"Some of them you wouldn't have believed when they first arrived," says Nick. "They looked shocking—most of the roof missing and things like that. I'm pretty pleased about what we were able to do with them. They're film props—they haven't had fourteen

An authentic early 1930s motorcycle painted with police insignia.

lacquers of paint baked on or anything like that, but they look good."

A special vehicles unit was established to paint the vehicles, convert them to left-hand drive, and get them into running order. Any that could not be mechanically revived were simply given a face-lift and positioned on set as parked cars.

Exterior features such as police and taxi lights were made by the props makers, as were license plates—about seventy pairs in all. Researcher Sarah Milnes had a stroke of luck when she turned to the Internet to find out what styles of plates and range of numbers would have been on vehicles in New York in the thirties. "She went into a chat room and asked anyone if they knew anything about number plates in New York 1930s, and some guy in New York happens to be writing a book about New York number plates in the thirties, so he responded with a whole lot of information," says Tony. A selection of appropriate numbers was then sent to Universal to go through a process of legal clearances. "Obviously we didn't want to be crashing some car that somebody's actually got that number plate for, so there was a lot of work involved in this historical correctness."

To dress the ship the *Venture*, many authentic fittings were sourced from England. "All the portholes, the ship's wheel, and the ship's lights—they were original salvaged bits off boats," says Phred, who bought the bulk of the originals through a naval salvage yard in the U.K. "There were so many boats—we had the interior, studio exterior, back-lot exterior, plus we had the real boat. To get matching sets of period ship's lights—we're talking about a couple of hundred lights by the time we did all the boats—that's tricky."

In fact, it is tricky to source matching sets of vintage anything—light shades, for instance, or door handles or freestanding ashtrays for the Empire State Building lobby. Says Phred, "If you're doing it from the States or U.K., you just go to the prop rental houses

Animal crates inside the *Venture* hold.

and you can get all those wonderful pieces. But they're not cheap, and shipping from the United States is so expensive. So we had things made. You might find one and then have that replicated by the props makers."

Among the nice little details the props makers created from scratch for the *Venture* is some animal excrement for the ship's hold, in many varieties, ranging from camel dung to mouse droppings, all thoroughly researched at Wellington Zoo. Ingredients included cocoa powder, gelatin, Weet-Bix (a breakfast cereal), mustard, and salt—almost good enough to eat.

"We're often referred to as the lie factory, the fib factory," says props maker Chris Streeter, who made a huge, fake industrial chain and pulley for the New York set that looks as if it should weigh a ton, but which can easily be picked up and moved around.

Carl Denham's movie

camera, a hand-cranked Bell & Howell, is just like the one the character uses in the 1933 *King Kong*. Nick was able to find someone who collects and restores old cameras and had the right Bell & Howell for sale. "It's a working camera," says Nick. "We had to do a little bit of stuff to adapt it, [but] we were able to make a camera that you could run film through. We were lucky enough to get our hands on a couple of the big thousand-foot magazines as well, the really big Mickey Mouse ears that go on top."

Actors who would be handling the camera on set were sent to Alex Funke, director of photography for visual effects, for training. "Alex is kind of an expert when it comes to old cameras and antique film equipment," says Jack Black, who plays film director Carl Denham. "He taught us how to put it together and film with this old camera. It was really fun, because it's all manual. You've got to be turning the thing at a precise motion, because if you go too fast, the image goes in slow motion, and if you go too slow, it looks like Babe Ruth running around the bases at the speed of light."

The actors got in some practice by making a couple of films with the camera—one criminal-on-the-

Kyle Chandler, John Sumner, and Jack Black with the Bell & Howell camera prop.

run movie and another called "The Boxer." "They're a minute-long, poor rendition of Keystone Kops," says Colin Hanks, who plays Denham's assistant, Preston.

"One of my favorite memories," he recalls, "is just picking up that camera the first time and realizing how heavy it was, and then all of us practicing running from dinosaurs, going, 'Dinosaurs, dinosaurs, we're running from dinosaurs,' and hoping that they'd come up with a good fake camera for us to use, because it is heavy!"

They did indeed come up with a fake camera, but it wasn't much lighter. Prop maker Simon Hames measured up the camera and made a wooden copy of it, which was then molded and cast in urethane.

Tony Drawbridge got to interact with a piece of movie history when he replicated some spears that had actually appeared in the original *King Kong*. "The spears that the Skull Islanders used as their weapons were bought by Peter in an auction," Tony explains. "I had to replicate them—obviously not taking a silicone mold off them, because that could potentially damage them or pull all the old paint off. Basically it was going round each one with a pair of calipers and measuring and eyeballing it." In an amusing twist, the replica spears are used in Peter Jackson's movie not by the Skull Island natives, but by the dancers who represent them at the Kong premiere in New York City.

Fake weapons for the *Venture* crew, and for the New York police and military officers, were made at Weta Workshop, where many are now on display. "Please feel free to take potshots," says Weta Workshop's Richard Taylor, waving toward a table piled with thirties-era pistols, rifles, and tommy guns. "They're all made of skateboard-wheel rubber—high-density urethane." He picks up a machine gun. "This is a First World War Lewis, total replica. There's nothing real on this table at all."

You'd be hard-pressed to spot the difference between these replicas and the real thing. The stocks look to be made of wood, the barrels of metal. And, like the replica camera, they're heavy. "We should really make them light so they're more comfortable for the actors, but we choose to weight them so that the actors feel like they've got real military weapons."

In some instances, the actors do have real weapons. If a shot calls for a sailor to cock the gun and pull the trigger, it is likely to be a real gun loaded with blanks. When the same sailor clambers through the jungle with the gun slung over his shoulder, the gun is a fake.

"I felt pretty confident with my tommy gun," says Jack Black, who got to fire his gun at an empty space that would eventually be filled with a digital creature. "I shoot a leviathan in the face, and it felt very satisfying. I think I looked really awesome doing it. Oh, and I shot my own raft to pieces"—he laughs—"and everyone got dunked in the water and some people died, but I did get that shot in the leviathan's face, right in his grille."

Actor Jed Brophy, who plays one of the *Venture* sailors, carried a rifle. "I wasn't lucky enough to get a tommy gun, although I wanted one. The rifles we had were authentic 1913 German Mauser 87s, and the ones that they made for us were just as heavy, and that actually added to it because when you're carting around big heavy ropes, heavy knapsacks, proper heavy torch, and a gun, you are exerted

Police-issue Smith and Wesson .38 revolvers, mass-produced in urethane for filming.

physically. It means you actually treat it like a real gun."

Qualified armorers and safety officers were always on set when the guns were used, and the actors were trained in safe practices. "We had brilliant armorers who would not let you get away with fooling around with even the pretend guns," says Jed. "They said, 'We'll take it off you, you'll be without a gun.' There was no misapprehension that you could fool around and point this gun at people . . . everybody treated even the nonreal guns as if they were weapons that could kill someone."

To give the fake guns a final touch of authenticity, Weta Workshop looked all over the world for a supply of the kind of webbing used to make gun straps for forces in World War I. "Our search brought us back to a company three hours north of Wellington, and they showed us the machine that actually wove the straps nearly one hundred years ago," says Richard. "The elderly gentleman said, 'Oh, I remember I had a key somewhere around here,' and literally

got a key out of the drawer, put it into the machine, and started it up. He's now woven ten thousand meters of webbing for us, on the original machine that made the ANZAC [Australia and New Zealand Army Corps] forces' webbing."

Richard estimates that a hundred or so replica guns were made for *King Kong*, plus knives and machetes. "Some of them are very wobbly," he says, picking up a rifle and flexing its barrel. "They're for putting on the backs of actors who have to fall over."

Machetes, likewise, were made of soft plastic for the scene in the pit, where the sailors are attacked by some digital slugs and crabs. The actors could swing the soft machetes around in a frenzied fashion without fear of dismembering each other. And hand grenades, realistically weighted so that they could be correctly thrown, were made soft and bouncy for safe landings. They all look so real.

"Go ahead," says Richard, laughing. "I dare you to pull the pin!"

Police-issue P14 rifles, reproduced in urethane.

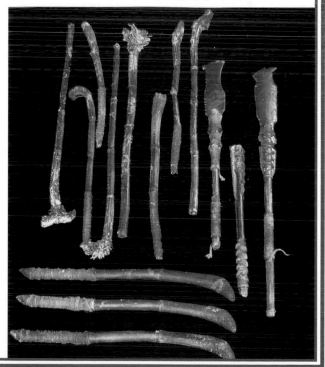

Native clubs, including the "hero" and two stunt versions of the club that Jack Driscoll is hit with.

A Curtiss Helldiver under construction.

One of the most famous images in movie history is from the original *King Kong*: that of Kong atop the Empire State Building, making his last stand against a fleet of biplanes. That iconic scene—and those biplanes—needed to be in Peter Jackson's version of *King Kong*, so the director hired aircraft consultant Gene DeMarco to build them.

The fighter planes in the original movie were crude replicas of Curtiss Helldivers, a type of biplane made by the Curtiss Aeroplane and Motor Company in Buffalo, New York. Gene's crew looked all over the world for surviving Helldivers, but none were to be found. So he tracked down the original drawings—which was not an easy task.

"I had to get a letter from the remains of the Curtiss company, Curtiss Wright, to give us permission to build airplanes using their drawings," he says. "But Curtiss doesn't have any [drawings]. They don't have archives; most of the drawings were left with the Smithsonian in Washington, D.C. I have a few good friends there, and they looked high and low and found out that there were no Curtiss Helldiver drawings at the Smithsonian."

Further research revealed that the drawings were actually in the American national archives, and Gene eventually managed to get copies, at considerable expense. Then came the challenge of reconstruction. "We took the fuselage drawing, which is the main body of the airplane and the structure, and we built an exact replica using different materials. So all the angles and all the tubes and all the structure is just like the real airplane. We even went to the extent of making sure that all the tubing inside the cockpit would be the same, so if Peter decided to shoot inside the airplane, or the instrument panels in the cockpit, it would be just like the original."

Not all the materials used in building the replicas are as they would have been on the original airplanes. Mild steel was substituted for chromelike moly tubing, and a round aluminum tube was used for the spars, rather than a built-up wooden spar. Many other parts, though, were manufactured to be just like the real thing. "We copied real parts, and the technicians we had here made them," says Gene.

"We've cheated a bit on tires—we've taken some old truck tires and shaved the tread off them to make them look like aircraft tires. We've even made some of our own instruments to look the period and fitted them into the instrument panel—primers and magneto switches and the actual flight instruments, like the altimeter and airspeed indicator. We have put some originals in there, but we were short on a few gauges, so we've made some from scratch."

FLYING ACES

The Helldivers date back to the days when aircraft were covered in fabric over a framework of wood and steel. "The originals would have used cotton or linen, but we've used a synthetic material," Gene says. "It's a lot like Dacron. You glue it on the structure and then you shrink it with heat. But it needs to be stitched in places, sewn on. We put the same reinforcing tapes on that you'd use in real airplanes." The finishing material for the fabric is called dope; it's similar to nail polish and makes the fabric shrink a little more so that the surfaces are tight.

One complication in the replication process was that the wings needed to be removable, to make it easier to get cameras in close. "Some of the shots Peter wanted were really unusual and evoke a lot of emotion," Gene explains. "He wanted to get closer to the pilots, and with wings in the way that would be quite difficult. Some of the close-ups and perspectives you couldn't really do in a flying airplane. Airplanes are notoriously complex things—you can't just take the wings off in twenty minutes. But the guys here are really good at thinking outside the square. It's wonderful when you come across that kind of skill where people say, 'Oh, we can find a way round that.'"

Gene and his crew built two Helldivers, although there appear to be more in the movie. Repainting numbers and markings makes them look different when required. The planes are mounted on gimbals that can make them tilt in different directions while the pilots operate the controls—which actually make the rudder and ailerons move.

One of the Helldivers even has a real engine in it, although it is not in running order. "We made a copy of that engine, and it's darn good—you can hardly tell the difference. In fact, most people can't tell the difference between the real engine and the copy," Gene says.

"There's been a huge effort to make everything as real as possible. Pete's an aviation fanatic, and he loves early airplanes, so we wanted to put as much detail into the airplanes as we could. You really wouldn't need to have all these working controls, but it just adds to the realism. A lot of the guns were real machine guns firing blanks, so they had the muzzle flash. Here's a guy, he's actually firing a real gun, so the expression on his face is that he's firing a real gun. The noise as he pulls the trigger, a bit of recoil . . . it's fantastic."

Fortunately Gene's crew don't have to crash their masterpieces for the final scenes in the movie—that's all done by Weta Digital, with advice from the aircraft experts. As opposed to the originals, these Helldivers could live on for a very long time.

Cockpit instrument panel for the Helldiver.

Top: A sign writer painting detail work on the Helldiver. Bottom: A Curtiss Helldiver relocated to set.

Left: Ann Darrow's silk slip as worn at her capture on board the *Venture*. This is stage one: clean and intact.
Top right: Jack Driscoll's silk shirt broken down in the final stage.
Lower right: Ann Darrow's silk slip broken down in the final stage.

There are dirty clothes on the racks in the costume department, and that's the way the costumiers like them. Making clothes dirty—in some cases, with six separate degrees of dirtiness—has been one of the key tasks for the *King Kong* costume designers.

"When the sailors do the chase on the island, they start clean and they've got to end absolutely devastated," Australian costume designer Terry Ryan explains. "So you work out that they've got, say, six stages of being dirty."

The sailors' shirts and trousers have had dirt permanently applied to them so it won't come out in the wash after a rough day on set. "We need to launder them, so they've got to come out looking just the same—only smelling better!" Terry says. "It's usually dyed and set to have that dirt in it, in that position, for the rest of its life."

The costumiers study the script to find opportunities to switch to the next degree of dirtiness, such as the scene in which the sailors get dumped into a swamp. "That's a perfect time to change them, so when they dry off they're dirtier or cleaner," says Terry.

So that's six shirts for each sailor, graded from relatively clean to absolutely devastated—but then the costumiers have to make multiple copies of each and every clean or dirty shirt! "There's the one they

wear, the stunt double's got to have one, and their picture double's got to have one. Then they've got to have a wet one and a dry one. . . . And you always have a spare just in case something goes horribly wrong. They could spill coffee on it. . . . You can't keep two hundred and fifty people waiting while you go and wash [a] stain out and wait for it to dry."

Naomi Watts spends much of the movie wearing a slip—or rather, one or another of many slips. "She's completely and absolutely vulnerable when she's on that island with Kong. She does the whole thing in that little pink satin slip. . . . She's got to climb up trees, fall down ditches, be chased by monsters, swing upside down. It has to be practical and still look great. Naomi's got twenty-eight slips. We're nearly running out of lace."

Little wonder then that the enormous costume department is crowded with row upon row of garment racks overflowing with hired, bought, or newly made 1930s clothing. But it's not all sailors' shirts and pink slips. The costume team had many hundreds of New Yorkers to dress, including theater patrons, dancers, military and police officers, down-and-out shantytowners, and everyday people on the streets—about two and a half thousand characters in all.

# COSTUMING FROM SCRATCH

62

Naomi Watts's slip costume underwent
a lot of manufactured wear and tear.

"Five hundred extras in New York," figures Terry, "and we dressed them three times each, so that's fifteen hundred. Each one of those extras had three costumes. They used them again in different places."

Then there was evening wear for the big Alhambra Theater scenes, filmed at the Civic Theatre in Auckland. "That was five hundred people," says Terry. "Two hundred and fifty of those were women and we manufactured most of those evening dresses . . . the vintage stuff is really small, so they don't fit anymore."

People today are, on average, larger than people in the 1930s. "They were really tiny back then," says Terry. "A woman was five foot two, with little size-six feet. And men were small—five foot eight with a thirty-eight-inch chest was quite average. Now it's forty-two inches and six foot."

At times, up to one hundred people worked in the costume department. Although some costumes were rented and accessories were bought from around the world, much was made in-house or made to order. Albion Clothing in Christchurch, New Zealand, made hundreds of suits. "We took vintage suits, drafted patterns off them, graded them to be contemporary sizes to fit contemporary bodies, then sent the patterns to them," says Terry. "We supplied the fabric and they manufactured them."

Finding fabrics with 1930s-style colors and prints is next to impossible, Terry says. You can't just run into a store and pick up some fabric. "We've got someone printing fabrics for us, dyeing colors. He's printing ties at the moment for the arty theater. It's its own department down by the front gate, dyeing and printing."

Another issue was color: as dyeing processes have become more sophisticated, colors have become sharper. "If you look at the vintage fabrics, they've got a dusky quality to them," says Terry. "But then you don't want it all dreary and downtrodden. We've had quite a lot of color discussion It's all gone back to those soft pastel colors—nothing too strong. It's the mood thing. We want the pretty girl who ends up taming the beast. You think she isn't going to do it, and then she pulls it off at the end, so she becomes a bit of a superwoman. Naomi wears pastels, lots of soft fabrics, nothing too hard—knits, overcoats of soft cashmere wool.

"She's in twinkly white velvet when Kong takes her up the Empire

Ann Darrow's glamorous beaded
dress for her film-within-a-film.
(All illustrations by costume
designer Terry Ryan.)

State Building. It's cut on the bias so, when the wind gets it, it ruffles. If you're going to put someone through all that hassle of standing in front of huge wind machines, you'd like their clothes to work in that environment."

Fabrics in the thirties tended to be of natural fibers: cotton, linen, wool, silk for evening wear. "There was a bit of rayon around. The good rayons you can't get. It's impossible to get good underwear silk. Adrien's shirt is in a great silk, but the only place that I've found it in the last twenty years is a place in Brisbane, Australia, and we've just used every inch of fabric they had—lovely shirting silk that you can't get anywhere [else]. People make it, but it's not the same, it hasn't got a weight, it doesn't drape.

"Everything's got to have a softness, even the tailored women's suits and the men's

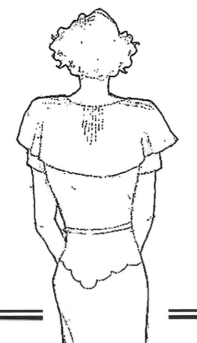

Front and back view of another of Ann's film-within-a-film dresses, this one for her scene with Bruce on the *Venture*

The clothing Jack wore during his unexpected voyage to Skull Island.

suits—they're not that nice, thin Italian fabric that people wear now. They've got bulk to them. The collars are thick. So that's the thing you're always saying: too thin, too thin, make it thicker."

Since the thirties was the time of the Great Depression in America, the clothing also needed to be "distressed." "Everything we've done has a process of making it look used," Terry says. "Americans call it distressing. It's just getting things so collars look a bit worn. It's sanding fabrics back, so they all soften up a bit and look like someone owns these clothes and they haven't just come out of a shop."

A buyer for the costume department scouted antique and vintage clothing shops around New Zealand for period jewelry, shoes, hats, and handbags. In addition, Kumfs, a New Zealand footwear company, made 330 pairs of period-style shoes for the women of New York. "The boys' shoes are okay because all those good English brands have been making those same shoes for the last hundred years," Terry says. "They're exactly the same—beautiful shoes."

A lot of men's hats were bought from Australian and American companies, while others were rented. "There's a company here called Hill's Hats that has been our lifesaver. They've made hundreds for us. They did mostly men's, and we've had a milliner in here full-time for quite a few months, churning out women's hats."

For Naomi's cloche hat

Naomi Watts models Ann Darrow's stunning cloche hat.

worn at the beginning of the film, several prototypes were made and tested. The costumiers worked with the hair and makeup department, balancing issues such as hair length, the period look, and photographic requirements. "You want a bit of mystery there, but you'd like to see some of the face if we shoot from the side," says Terry. "Everything's tested before it goes in front of the big camera. We did weeks of wardrobe and makeup tests on camera, trying all the different filters, all the different light sources—sunrise and sunset, nighttime, stormy, wet, dry, what the actors look comfortable in or look good in."

Jack Black was by far the easiest actor to get looking just right. "He put everything on and he just made it work," says Terry. "There was a minimum of fuss. He comes in with no preconceived idea of how he's going to look. So when you say, 'This is what we were thinking,' Jack will put it on and say, 'Oh, I can make this work.' So he then takes on his new skin. That's why he's so good. He is. He's pretty fantastic."

A terrifying rat-a-tatting noise suddenly thunders out from the studio just across the alley. "It's gunfire," says assistant costume designer Eliza Godman. "They're shooting Kong. It scared me to death the other day."

Next on the filming schedule is the

Ann's costume for the streets of New York City.

64

Jack Black models the finished Carl Denham Skull Island costume.

premiere of Jack Driscoll's play at the "arty theater," where a cultured audience needs to be dressed in sophisticated, slightly quirky tailored styles.

"It's like a couture house here," says Terry. "Everything's toile, everything's fitted, everything's changed over and over again. . . . Those dresses are blown up to a hundred times their size onscreen . . . you don't get away with a safety pin."

The costume for Carl Denham on Skull Island, which was eventually broken down in stages.

Naomi Watts's wigs for the movie were styled in a loose, but still authentic, fashion.

Peter King has a room full of blood. He also has plentiful supplies of scabs, mud, grime, and engine oil. It's all part of the paraphernalia he needs as makeup and hair designer for *King Kong*.

Lots of blood and mud is required for the scenes of mayhem on Skull Island, and the *Venture* crew always have to look like a rough lot. But the movie covers such a wide range of scenes and people that the makeup team has had to be prepared for anything, from bloody sailors to New York socialites.

Peter's main priority, though, has been Naomi Watts. As the central character, Ann Darrow, her look for the film was a key topic during his early planning with Peter Jackson and Fran Walsh. They needed to make her look right for the period, right for her character, and right for the audience. They also wanted her to look a little like Fay Wray in the original film. It has been quite a balancing act.

## MAKING UP AND WIGGING OUT

"I had a meeting with Peter and Fran and the producers, discussing what we wanted our principals to look like," Peter says. "Naomi's character is the only woman amongst a band of men. Although we're making a period film, we wanted to make her look more soft and vulnerable. The 1930s is quite a coiffured look, and it could be considered to be quite a hard look, so we didn't want to make her look terribly fashionable. We had to make sure that people were prepared to go along with her story.

"People associate certain looks with certain emotions. A lot of 1930s style is really quite painted, and that suggests someone quite hard, with the thin eyebrows and the lashes and the lipstick. I did do some drawings early on of Naomi with very thin eyebrows. . . . I'd plucked her eyebrows out and I'd drawn new ones on, and reshaped her mouth and did a real classic thirties thing with her, with waved hair. It looks incredibly hard . . . you'd have thought this woman would have just got hold of Kong, swung him around her head, and chucked him.

"[Instead] We came up with a very soft look for Ann Darrow that had the feeling of the period, but it was a little more like she was almost an out-of-towner . . . someone who might be onstage but wasn't like a lot of the hardened girls who were there."

In comparison, the male actors have been easy—just a little light makeup for the principals, nothing at all for the extras. The *Venture* crewmen start out looking rough and get even rougher during their hellish ordeal on the island. That's where Peter's blood and mud come in.

"Blood and mud you can either make

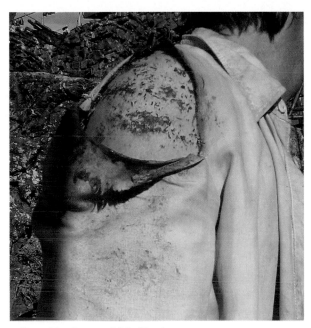

Peter King's special fake blood mixture is quite convincing.

or buy," he says. "We've got a whole room next door full of different types of blood, whether be it congealed, fresh, runny, arterial, or other types of blood, so it's dark red, light red, orange-red. Then we have fresh scab, which is what you put on to look like the wound has just healed over, but it's still fresh, congealed blood.

"Mud, we make ourselves, out of children's powder paints, mixed with water or with aloe vera gel and some baby lotion. We use different pigments, depending on whether you want real mud or runny mud or oily mud or whatever. I had to make engine oil for this movie. Engine oil's great—it's castor oil and glycerin and some pigment, just shaken up, and you put it on skin and it looks like this very greasy, awful black oil."

Fake tans are made out of aloe vera gel and food coloring. Sunburn calls for more red and yellow to produce an orange effect, and a little green adds a

Naomi Watts and Adrien Brody with the soft, natural look designed by Peter King.

dirty tinge. The gel is transparent so that any spots or marks on the skin underneath it remain visible. And the dirt, grease, and tans don't wash off when the actors get tons of water thrown over them.

Some of the required makeup was a bit more decorative: "We did a lot of tattoos," says Peter. "We did a lot of researching into tattoos of the period and came up with strange Indonesian ones . . . the boat is registered in Surabaya in the film, so it's all Indonesia and Java. . . . I found all these tattoos from the nineteenth century, from different places, and amalgamated them, so it's a big mishmash. One sailor has *H-O-L-D F-A-S-T* on his knuckles. There's a whole tradition of tattoos for sailors, and they all mean certain things."

Peter uses the Internet for his research these days. The walls of the makeup room are covered in printouts of images he's found of the 1930s. He has scrapbooks in different categories: burlesque, Depression people, young ladies, uptown, downtown, shantytown. . . .

"At the very beginning of the film there's a montage shot where we had to do all of the down-and-outs, the soup kitchens, the people who run illicit stills being taken away by police. Our notion of the 1930s is in black and white, from newsreels and images and a lot of the films from those days. For us to see something that's correct for the period, but it's in bright Technicolor, in some ways it looks wrong. So I decided early on, with Terry upstairs, to keep all those streets, all the outside stuff, really colorless. I had hardly anyone in makeup, even in uptown, to try and pull it back."

There are hundreds of extras in the film. Casting helps here; they try to look for suitable faces, such as craggy faces for the poor and out-of-work people in New York. Peter prefers to let such faces speak for themselves, without his intervention.

"I always say, when I've done lectures and stuff,

the first thing when you're designing something is, decide whether people are going to wear makeup or not. And people are astounded and say, 'Surely everyone wears makeup?' And I say, 'No, they don't, not at all.' What's the point putting makeup on someone if they've got to look quite depressed or down and out?

"You could do a whole film without any makeup. . . . People have the idea that everyone gets caked in stuff. I only use makeup where people would be wearing makeup. So uptown women would be wearing powder and lipstick and have their eyebrows done, but women downtown might have . . . a red blotchy face with a bit of lipstick on. Or, if they're working women who've been gutting fish or selling apples, they wouldn't put makeup on, so you don't put makeup on them. No extra men have makeup on at all."

It is in the uptown theaters of the film's final scenes that Peter King and his team could finally let loose with the more glamorous look of the 1930s. For those who could afford it, the 1930s was a time of fashion conformity. People wanted to look like Hollywood stars.

"It's very different now because up until the seventies there was a fashion, and that's basically what you followed," says Peter. "I can remember when platform shoes came back in, that's all you really could buy unless you went to an old lady's shop. Nowadays it's so diverse, there is no one style, there is no fashion of the period. There are influences, but it's not like it was up until the sixties and slightly into the seventies where you had 'This is *the* look.' . . . It's amazingly diverse now.

"A lot of the thirties look was set down by Hollywood, the films they were making and all the glamorous people, like Jean Harlow, Marlene Dietrich, and

*Jack Black's hair was tucked under a wig for his portrayal of Carl Denham.*

Greta Garbo. And people aspired to them like young people aspire now to rock stars and musicians and hip-hop bands. So all the people pouring into the theater for the first night of Kong onstage, very ritzy people, very glamorous—everything is satin, drop-dead dresses, and all this fabulous, coiffured, waved hair, and lots of diamonds and furs, which was great fun. And all those thin eyebrows—that's a very good look for the period. We've been doing a lot of plucking. So when you come back from all that's happened on the island, it's a real culture shock."

To come up with the makeup design for the native-dance number at the Kong premiere, Peter had to look no further than the 1933 version of *King Kong.* "We used the makeup from the natives in the

original film as the basis for the makeup on [the dancers]," he says. "It was all very bad stage makeup, deliberately very badly done."

When it comes to doing the hair for a movie, Peter likes to bring his own. Back home in Britain, he runs his own wigmaking company with partner Peter Owen, and he believes there are many advantages to putting wigs on actors' heads. Not only does it enable him to get exactly the look he wants—which an actor's own hair might not suit—but it also saves a lot of time and hassle on the set.

Naomi is one of those who wears wigs in the movie—blond and curly. "Her natural hair is straight," says Peter. "It would have been tortured every day and she would have spent hours in the chair getting ready. Wigging is what I'm sort of famous for, anyway. So we decided to wig her—one, because it looks after her own hair, and two, it's much quicker to do. It would be two hours doing her hair, whereas it takes half an hour to pop a wig on."

Actor Jack Black also has his own hair tucked under a wig as he transforms into Carl Denham. "Peter Jackson had this great idea that Denham ought to be Orson Wellean in look," says Peter. "He sent me some pictures of Orson Welles and loved the sort of megalomaniac look of him, this fabulous waved hair with all those bits hanging down. We tried cutting Jack's hair at first, we even permed it, but it didn't work . . . so again we wigged."

Peter defies any audience to spot the difference between his wigs and real heads of hair on-screen. For a start, all of Peter's wigs are made of real human hair. He pulls out a wig and turns it inside out, revealing the skin-colored lace beneath. It takes a skilled wigmaker about three or four weeks to knot each hair into the lace—maybe twenty thousand hairs to a wig, he estimates. "We color and mix the hair to make them look as real as possible. There would be about seven different colors in this head of

hair, and it would be slightly darker at the back and lighter in the front—anything to make it look more real." The hairs thin out toward the hairline, leaving an edge of bare lace that gets glued to the actor's skin. He lays the forehead edge against the back of his hand. Even without a covering of makeup, the fine, pale lace is almost invisible against his skin.

Naomi has three wigs for the movie, all the same, which can be styled according to the needs of each scene. "You've always got them dressed into style and standing by. If she's on set and they change to a new scene, it might mean she's got to go to a different look, so you just take one wig off and put another one on. Or it gets so wrecked that you can't use it anymore, so you put another one on and it doesn't hold the camera up too long."

Providing wigs for hundreds of extras was a special challenge. In the 1930s the fashionable look for women was short, wavy hair. In the 1920s it was the bob. But not every woman was a follower of fashion. Some wore styles dating back to the 1910s or 1900s. "Some of the older ladies, when they go and see Kong in the theater, they've got long hair that's waved up, rather than short hair," says Peter. "Getting that whole mix, getting it feeling right—you can fit every single person, wigs on nearly everyone, and then you go, 'Oh, no, there's too many of those looks together, we'll change that. Is the balance right? Does it look believable?'"

Some of the more elegantly scalloped hairstyles on the wigs displayed on the makeup room shelves look as if they could have been lifted straight from the heads of the most glamorous socialites and film stars of the 1930s, but there is nothing sophisticated about the tools Peter and his team use to achieve the kinks and waves—just fingers and water. "It's finger-waving. That's what they did in that period, they didn't use rollers," says Peter. "You finger-wave the hair with water on your fingers. All of these little, tiny, tight waves were done by just pushing the hair with your fingers and a comb."

Finger-waving—for women and men—came into vogue as a means of controlling permed hair, which was a relatively new invention back in the thirties. "Everyone had perms," explains Peter. "It was the era of the perm. They had this wonderful system of connecting themselves up to electricity to produce heat that would permanently wave their hair. But then you had a big shock of curly hair, which was . . . completely uncontrollable. So that's how finger-waving came about really, as a way of controlling the hair and putting all these waves in."

Pin-curling was another handy trick: "That's where you get little, tiny bits of hair and you wrap it round your finger and you put two cross pins in it. We did thousands of them. That's what all women used to go through, all these famous film stars."

Not all of the cast of *King Kong* wear wigs—Adrien Brody, for instance. "We just cut his hair," says Peter, "not too 1930ish. We wanted to make it look a bit outgrown, like he really doesn't bother, like the hassled young writer with all these bits sticking up. So he was quite easy really."

Then there was the *Venture* crew, a rough lot who needed a rough look—not just for their hair, but also for their beards, mustaches, or stubble. "They all had to look a bit scuzzy, especially Andy Serkis, who's the cook. We had him [look] really, really rough." Peter

Adrien Brody's hair was cut and styled to look disheveled, as befitting a preoccupied young writer.

laughs. "He turned up with a full beard, and we shaved the beard off, left stubble, and left his mustache."

Of course, with all the action on Skull Island, many of the actors have stunt doubles, and the doubles have to have hair that looks exactly like the actors. "We've had to double all the crew. We've had to double some of the doubles, we've had to stunt-double and body-double . . . we were having different people coming in every day because they couldn't get people who could do the whole week. So, put a wig on him . . . no, color his hair . . . no, he was so-and-so yesterday but he's going to be somebody else today . . . It got quite confusing in places."

Peter would not recommend asking your hair-

dresser to color your hair the way he colors his wigs: in a boiling saucepan. "You'd have a bit of a burnt scalp." He laughs. "I don't use hair dye, we use fabric dyes. Hair dye ruins the hair because it's got so many chemicals in it. We just do it with fabric dye and boiling water. . . . We dye it in great big pans and we use dyes designed for dyeing wool. Our hair is exactly the same basically, it's a natural fiber. And it's great [dye] because it doesn't destroy the hair at all, and you get nice clear colors.

"A lot of the time we precurl the hair, which is like perming it, but again we don't use perm lotion, we use boiling water, which permanently curls it. People could do that if they stick their head in boiling water as well."

Andy Serkis as Lumpy the cook.

Full-size exterior *Venture* set on the backlot at Stone Street Studios.

The S.S. *Venture* is tied up at Miramar Wharf, not far from Wellington Airport. It looks like a nineteenth-century tramp steamer, but underneath its grungy, rust-bucket exterior is the *Manuia*, a Dutch fishing boat and trader, built in the 1950s.

"I'd been hunting around for a ship, phoning everyone I knew in various ports around the country," says Dan Hennah, supervising art director. "I was asking about any ships that might look like the one in the original *King Kong*. I'd seen the *Manuia* fifteen years ago and thought, 'Wow, that's a particular type of freighter that just doesn't exist anymore.' I spoke to a friend in Tauranga, who said, 'I'm driving past it right now—it's tied up at the wharf.' I flew up, went on board, and had a look, and the owner was ready to sell. So we got lucky.

"It had just come in from fishing up off Tonga in the central Pacific, and it had forty tons of frozen tuna on board, but couldn't unload in New Zealand because of regulations about where it had caught the fish. But when the owner was able to prove that he'd sold it out of the fishing industry, the New Zealand government let him off-load into containers and transship his fish. So we got it without the fish, thank goodness."

"It needed radical changing," says production designer Grant Major. "The

## MARITIME MAKEOVER

movie is set in 1933, and the *Venture* is an old boat by then—manufactured perhaps sometime around the late 1800s. Back then, it would have had a vertical bow . . . but the *Manuia* had a curved bow. One of the first things we wanted to get right was its silhouette. So we managed to straighten up the bow by this spectacular piece of steelwork that was done with the boat still in the water."

"We ballasted it," Dan explains. "We took water ballast out of the forward end and put [it] down the stern, to ballast the bow up out of the water. We welded on our new bow—just added a piece over the top—and then filled it up with ballast again."

The upper decks also had a makeover. "The *Manuia* has the bridge at the back, and the front has a longer cargo-hold area," says Grant. "We wanted the *Venture* to be a multipurpose boat, with a cargo hold as well as being a passenger transport." The original bridge was transformed into Denham's cabin, and more cabins and a wheelhouse were added in front of it.

The layout of the ship was inspired more by the script than by any real-world ship design. "It had to have a bridge, the captain's cabin, Ann's cabin, and Bruce's cabin. It had to have connecting corridors inside and a mess, and it had to have the top deck areas where various dialogue

Jack Driscoll's "tiger cage" sleeping quarters.

The *Venture*'s hold interior with animal cages.

scenes would happen," says Grant. "So it was a jigsaw puzzle of all these individual scripted pieces, built into a ship."

The script dictated some aesthetic touches as well. "The invented history of the *Venture*," says Grant, "is that Englehorn uses it as a boat for importing animals into New York, hence it's full of cages—on top decks and belowdecks. It gives weight to the fact that the boat is geared up for transporting Kong back to New York, perhaps. And because Jack [Driscoll] wasn't scheduled to be part of the crew, he's living in the tiger's cage, down in the hold.

"There's a humorous aspect to that, but I see an

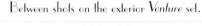

Between shots on the exterior *Venture* set.

animal cruelty thing to it as well. There was a big importation of animals from around the world back then—they just snatched them out of the jungles and put them in zoos. . . . So there's this thing about animals in cages and the feelings that those images conjure up."

Despite all of this work on the ship itself, most of the scenes set on the *Venture* were not in fact filmed on the *Manuia*. The ship's interiors were all built as individual sets at Stone Street Studios, and another *Venture* set was built on the back lot, surrounded on three sides by blue screen to facilitate special effects shots. And all the sets had to have a specific look.

"It had to look like an old dunger of a boat," says set finishing supervisor Kathryn Lim, whose team had the task of weathering the *Manuia* and the back-lot *Venture* exteriors. "It had to look like it was painted steel with layers and layers of peeling paint,

like the paint has come off but they've not tried to tidy it up, the next year they've just painted over it again. We plastered it to give it a pitty profile, and then we painted. It's really only one layer of paint, but it's been thickened with an acrylic thickener. The rust we created with oxide powders and shellac, or a regular acrylic stain, strategically placed. It gives the feeling it's been here for ages, that the water's seeped up, it's leaching minerals, and it's really gross."

The back-lot boat and many of the studio sets were built on a huge, hinged steel frame so that they could be tilted as needed to simulate movement at sea. "If you shoot ship sets on a gimbal, which lets you move the ship, after about half an hour everyone gets seasick," says Dan. "You get a much more effective ship-at-sea movement in-camera, using little tricks to swing the lights and tilt the water in the jug.

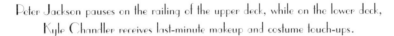

Peter Jackson pauses on the railing of the upper deck, while on the lower deck, Kyle Chandler receives last-minute makeup and costume touch-ups.

In addition to that, you can tilt the set. It's still stationary, but it has a tilt on the floor, so people have to walk uphill one way and downhill the other way. That helps the illusion that the ship is heeling over, or it's hard up on a rock. You're much better off to trick it than to try and do it for real!"

Once filming on the back-lot *Venture* was completed, the set was dismantled. "We put the very stern of the vessel in the studio with the interior sets, so that you could have the doors open and look out from the galley, along the corridor, and out over the stern," says Dan. "The wheelhouse and the forward cabins went onto the *Manuia*." Part of the dock set was set up beside the *Manuia* at Miramar Wharf, for shots of the *Venture* moving away from the wharf in New York.

Once its filming days are done, what will become of the *Manuia*? "There are all sorts of wonderful ideas for what you could do with it," says Dan. "One of them would be to set the *Venture* up as a museum piece, as a piece of film history, in the shallow water at Greta Point here in Wellington. It's a perfect spot for it."

Adrien Brody with director of photography Andrew Lesnie on the *Venture* set.

*Venture exterior set on Stone Street Studios backlot, with a view of Miramar Heights above the blue screen.*

VENTURE
SURABAYA

Fully dressed interior *Venture* studio set of the ship's galley, where Lumpy "cooks."

Walking from the art department to the interior sets of the *Venture* takes longer than necessary for set dressing supervisor Tanea Chapman. She just can't seem to walk past any set without spotting work to be done.

"Look!" she cries, pausing in the foyer of the Empire State Building, where a member of her team is polishing the floor. "The painters have done an incredible job—all this wonderful marbling. They've worked really long and hard for weeks to get this right. And now every Tom, Dick, and Harry is walking all over it!" She laughs. Hence the need for diligent polishing. "On camera that marbling is going to look fantastic."

Outside the "arty theater," where a well-disciplined audience of extras is laughing uproariously at a performance of Jack Driscoll's latest play, there is a mess of sun-bleached dinosaur bones. "Our job is to put the props in the set," explains Tanea. "Sometimes the props are furniture and curtains, sometimes the props are spiderwebs and stegosaur skeletons. We have to figure out which order this skeleton goes. I had Alex, the guy who made these things, come and lay it out for us beautifully, but in the interim somebody's moved them all."

Finally she reaches her destination: Studio B, a large shed that was once home to *The Lord of the Rings* Bag End sets, but which now houses a long row of *Venture* interiors. From the outside, they look like nothing more than an assortment of large black packing cases.

Tacked onto the end of one of these packing cases is the exterior of the ship's stern. "This was originally out on the back lot," says Tanea. She rattles off a bewildering explanation of which bits of the *Venture* were built where, and to where they were later moved. "We all struggle," she says, laughing. "Which bit of the boat are we dressing? Which boat? And then we have the interior sets of the boat, but not the whole boat, just a bit of the boat."

Most of the ship's surfaces are simply painted to look like particular kinds of old wood or rusting metal, but the decking outside the ship's mess is made of real (and therefore costly) jarrah wood. Tanea dismisses the idea that the decking could just have been painted as well. "If it's all fake, it feels fake, but if you combine real and really good fake, it stays looking real."

We follow our noses down a rabbit-warren corridor to the ship's tiny galley. It looks the epitome of grunge, with battered pots and pans, a food-stained sink and stove, and filth in every nook and cranny. "It absolutely stinks in here!" exclaims Tanea. "We've got Chinese herbs

# DRESSING THE VENTURE

and stinky fish. The cook on the ship supposedly picks up exotic things from port to port, so we've dressed his kitchen with lots of smelly things—not meaning to make it smelly, but they just are by default. We put all the veggies in before they needed them, so by the time they did need them they looked grotty [grungy, unpleasant] and horrible, because that's what they would look like. We use various spices and just chuck them around, and bits lie in the corners."

In Ann's cabin, Tanea points out a once ornate wardrobe mirror. "One of our props buyers, Melissa, this is her parents' mirror from their house, and lots of the silver has come off the back. It's just brilliant, because it sells the cabin as ugly and grotty. . . . You

get such depth of character with something grotty like that."

Tanea flips down something that appears to be a porcelain bowl standing on its side, but which is actually a foldaway hand basin. "It's a ship-style thing. They fold up, and the tap fits just inside the bowl. As you close it, it tips your dirty water down the back of the cabinet and out into the drain. It's modeled off one from Wellington's Maritime Museum—the whole design was replicated."

Bruce's cabin doubled as Preston's cabin. "The idea was that most of the cabins on the boat look the same, so we just changed the dressing. They're pretty pokey and nasty." Tanea laughs. "The mattresses are just a cover and we've filled them with furniture blan-

*Ann's cabin aboard the* Venture.

kets to make them look lumpy and uncomfortable.

"Our props buyer Phred found a shop that had beautiful, beautiful vintage linen. But then we take these pristine, heavy, gorgeous linen sheets and we have to dye them brown and dirty and rub holes in them. It's criminal!"

Inside Denham's cabin, a set of stairs leads down to nowhere. "This was the first set we dressed, when the set dressers first started," says Tanea. "Our job is to take all the props and integrate everything. We'll put ash in the ashtrays—just final touches that make it look like a real place rather than a set.

"The bulkhead lights are real period fittings. The portholes are real, made of brass, but they didn't have latches or lids, so the prop makers made those out of

plastic. . . . [Leslie] does a lot of fabric props, so she'd make all the curtains and tablecloths. But then we sat there with sandpaper and knocked them back and bleached the ends to make them look like they'd been there for ages. The same for the windows—Grant, the production designer, wanted the windows to look salt-crusted. So we mixed beer and salt together, and it dissolves at such a rate that you just paint the window and it does this lovely crystallized thing.

"It's really hard [work]," Tanea says, "but it's so variable and that's why we all like it. That's the charm of the job. You never know what you're going to be doing next."

And off she breezes, to deal with more of the countless tasks in need of her attention.

The *Venture*'s communal bathroom, fully dressed.

Top and bottom: Pummelling the *Venture* with manufactured waves.

As special effects coordinator, Steve Ingram's job is to unleash the elements on cast and crew. He and his team have soaked them with rain, engulfed them in steam, drenched them with stormy seas, and every day, for seven months, blasted them with wind, wind, and more wind.

"Pete was adamant that Skull Island was going to be windy," says Steve. Consequently, the main, second, and miniatures units have all had to endure the breezy weather. Wherever there are lights and cameras, there are fans of all sizes, from large to enormous, mounted on fork hoists, dollies, and scaffolding. "It's worth setting up to do atmosphere every shot," Steve insists, "even though it drives you crazy."

"It's a bit like living on a bus stop," adds first assistant director Carolynne Cunningham. "After the first six months you don't notice it."

Battering the *Venture* exterior with violent weather made for some memorable working conditions out on Stone Street Studios' back lot. In addition to the inevitable wind machines, the special effects team hung a rain bar (an arrangement of big aluminum pipes with spray nozzles) from a crane and pumped water through it to rain over the boat, while a dozen dump-tanks sent waves crashing over the ship's decks. The tanks, mounted on three movable scaffolding towers, each hold about a ton and a half of water. On cue, the water is tipped violently down a chute to a "kicker," or scoop, which then sends it surging back upward to splash over the boat.

"If you just dumped tons of water on someone, you'd probably kill them," says Steve. "But if it's going into the kicker, a lot of the energy is dissipated and it's aerated and turned into foam. It looks like a whole mass of water, but it goes over you quite easily."

"We try to get it so it just hits the top edge of the deck, so it breaks realistically. Years ago we used three-ton tanks. You get this big splash of water, then it disappears. A wave has a lot of mass behind it, so we found that by splitting it into two tanks, and triggering one slightly after the other, it looks more realistic."

The *Venture* exterior was stationary, but could be hoisted onto a tilt to look as if it had run aground and to give the actors an off-kilter look. Any sense of the live-action set pitching and rolling is pure illusion, created by the movement of cameras and actors. "When they roll cameras and the first wave crashes, everyone will lurch and then stumble up," says Steve. "Caro Cunningham barks a few cues at them on the loud-hailer: 'Fall! Waves hitting now!'—although it's pretty hard to hear when there's so many wind machines going and we're making it rain and we've got dump-tanks going.

# MAKING WAVES

Crew members try to stay dry while the *Venture* is drenched.

"Nobody stays dry. Even Peter gets wet. He doesn't mind. You look around and he's usually in amongst it somewhere. It's great for the actors to be in there too. Often in films it would be stunt doubles, but we had the actors right in the waves. You could tell they were really energized by it all. It's quite a feeling to be standing in front of a couple of tons of water and you hear the clank of the tank as it releases and then it all shoots down. It's exciting."

"It was fantastic!" says New Zealand actor Jed Brophy, who portrays the *Venture* crewman he named Skeggs. "The water was actually bowling you off your feet and there was a fair amount of drama involved. Andy Serkis [Lumpy the cook] did actually fall off the boat, but they had a big safety net down there, so he didn't get hurt."

"Andy was throwing something overboard right as he got hit by a wave," recalls Jack Black, who plays Carl Denham. "And then, when the wave stopped and he threw the thing overboard, he had too much momentum and he flipped over the end of the boat. But luckily Andy Serkis is a legendary, world-class athlete and emerged unharmed—legend!"

Between takes, a fire engine was on hand to refill the dump-tanks. "We can fill all twelve tanks in about seven minutes—generally by the time the actors have dried off and are ready to go again," says Steve.

Carolynne reckons cast and crew take such rigors as the repeated drenchings in their stride: "It's just people making waves on a big tank out on the back lot. What's so abnormal about that?" She laughs. "Can you imagine trying to shoot something like that on a real location . . . it'd be a nightmare!"

Although most of the sea in the movie will be crafted by Weta Digital, Carolynne says Steve's waves will help sell the effects. "You need to try the best you can to make it look like something's happening out there, because the crashing interactive waves are very hard for Digital. Otherwise it would look like we were filming in a swimming pool, which of course we were."

A wet set, much like a swimming pool, was built on the same back lot where the exterior *Venture* had stood. It was about sixty yards wide, surrounded by blue screen and filled to a depth of three feet with heated, chlorinated water. Several locations were built in the wet set, including the swamp and the entrance to Skull Island.

Creating some gentler waves to lap against Skull Island's rocky shore was an unexpected challenge for the special effects team. Originally not planned as a special effect, the team had little time to figure out how to do it.

Opposite page, top: Overhead view of a wet set.
Below: Skull Island's rocky coastline.

"We had a week to do it in," says Steve. "So we came up with an idea of getting some big excavators, and we took off their buckets and attached some steel platforms that we then put in the water and moved. It splashed a lot of water out of the wet set, but it made believable waves. . . . We did three of them so we could synchronize them. We grabbed one guy from the greens department, one of our special effects guys, and a builder, to drive them. We brought them in a day early to do a bit of rehearsing. So in the end we had the actors rowing to shore, the platforms in the water—in sequence, all cued together—making waves, plus some off-kilter rotating drums making a chop on the surface of the water. And wind, of course. It was great!"

Some of the whaler shots were done indoors against a sea of green screen, with the boat on a motion-control rig—also the responsibility of the special effects team. "We took the boat with twelve people out in the rough sea and took some markers on how it was moving and how they were rowing," says Steve. "Then we programmed some moves that would make our boat on the motion base do the same sort of movements. The boat's not in the water—it's on a hydraulic platform that can rotate forty-five degrees in any direction. The shot will have digital sea added later, but we programmed water mortars, which blast water out on cue, so when the boat dips down and the camera is in a certain posi-

tion, a burst of water will splash up over the bow and over the actors.

"The raft in the swamp had to bump and then be picked up and pushed along by the swamp creature. For when it first gets hit, we put some cables on the raft and pulled it across the water in the wet set. When we needed the actors and stunt doubles to be flicked up and fall off, we did that on a blue screen with the raft on a rig."

Jed was one of the actors on the first raft. "They attached the raft with a cable to a big digger, which then pulled it to make it look like the monster had come up underneath and lifted it, and it was actually quite scary," he says. "It was quite a vehement tug by this machine. And we all did lose our balance, so we didn't actually have to act that part. I got to do a kind of a big Hollywood fall in the water—fantastic!" He laughs. "We were all in the water, which was about twenty-nine degrees [Celsius]. We were in that for the best part of three or four days."

"Sadly this film has been very taxing for the cast," says Carolynne, "because they are either being dragged through the water or stuck in front of a blue screen on some mats with the wind being driven at them. But it's an action film, that's what happens, and they were all up for it. Our safety guys have looked after everyone really well and we've had a masseuse come in to give massages. But the actors are great. They've really taken it in their stride."

Shooting the whaler against a green screen.

Miniature (1:12 scale) *Venture*, seen from midship.

It's enough to make one feel seasick, watching the miniature *Venture* pitching and rolling.

The miniatures unit is preparing to do one of dozens of shots of the ship. Sweeping camera moves past the model will show the *Venture*'s progress at various stages of its voyage. The sea will be added in post-production, so this ship model is high and dry on a motion rig.

"On this rig, we can control three axes," explains Weta Workshop modelmaker/model technician Fraser Wilkinson. "We've got yaw, which screws the boat around on the spot; the pitch, which is the seesaw action of the boat; and the roll, from side to side. For each shot, Weta Digital will give us coordinates for how the boat needs to move and where the camera should be in relation to the boat, so we can mimic the motion of the boat through water."

Fraser was one of a team of Weta Workshop modelmakers who, under the leadership of Rebecca Asquith, spent more than six months building the miniature boat, and he is now looking after it on the shooting stage. At fourteen feet long, the miniature is one-twelfth the size of the full-scale seafaring *Venture*. "It's made of mainly timber. There's a steel frame inside. The hull is diagonal planked plywood and any other things we could find that would do the job—bits of wire, a lot of styrene and acrylic."

## MINI VENTURE

The detailing is exquisite and a near-perfect match for the full-scale version, right down to the rust and rivets. Fraser recalls only too well the painstaking task of putting hundreds of rivets onto the ship. The model-makers used a flatbed laser cutter to cut tiny rivet shapes into a sheet of self-adhesive vinyl, then picked them off the sheet with a strip of sticky tape. "We could lay lines of these little vinyl heads onto the hull about thirty at a time."

Miniature cargo crates were also cut by laser. The anchor chain was made by a 3D rapid prototyper, a kind of computer printer, which miraculously prints out three-dimensional physical models. But most features were made by hand or molded and cast from handcrafted models. "The team use whatever materials will do the job," says Fraser. "If a cotton reel will do for the end of a drum, it's a cotton reel we'll use."

Not all of the boat's doors and windows open. An open door means the interior has to be detailed. "We've got full detail in the wheelhouse. You can see right through it, so we've got all of the instruments, including a telegraph, which has lights and wording on the panel."

The exterior lights are perfect scale replicas of the real exterior bulkhead lights that were around in the period. They were cast in bronze, and the textured glass for them was blown into a mold. "Peter

92

Opposite page, top: Bridge of the miniature *Venture*.
Below: Miniature *Venture* sits in the Weta Workshop parking lot, ready to travel to the set.

wanted to see more splashes of light onto the walls, so we had to hide more lights inside the ship. Using an aluminum tube, which is polished on the inside, I made a focusable little spotlight, tiny scale, about five millimeters across, which throws quite a major light out so it could light up the back of the funnel and down onto various deck areas."

Each of the miniature's 120 or so lights can be individually switched on or off or dimmed. If Carl Denham is burning the midnight oil while everyone else onboard is asleep, the lighting on the miniature will be switched accordingly.

The stage lighting is kept relatively dim, so it will not wash out the effect of the miniature's tiny lights. Today's shots will show the ship at dawn, with an early-morning wash of light on one side. "It's quite a low light, so we can't shoot at high speed," says Fraser. "We need to be able to have the camera shutter open for a little while for this light to make an impression on the film, so it means we have to shoot at really, really slow speeds. For a low-light camera pass of, say, one hundred and fifty frames, which will be only a few seconds on-screen, it might take up to half an hour to shoot one pass."

On a nearby bench is a replica of a small section of the ship's prow. It is severely dented. "There's a sequence as they approach Skull Island where they ram the seawall," says Fraser. "From then on, we need to show that it's a bit bent-up. So just this morning, I've cut the bow of the ship off. I'll do a bit of a repaint whenever I swap the bows over, but I've gotten pretty used to painting it now. We've done a lot of touch-ups along the way."

Fraser loved building model aircraft as a kid and had cars and train sets. "I never suspected that I'd be able to do it for a job and end up here, doing this. This is the best job in the world, eh?"

93

View of the miniature stern.

The miniature *Venture* sitting atop a motion rig.

Ann and Jimmy dancing on the *Venture*'s deck. The live action was shot inside the studio, and a digital ocean and sky were added

Early on in *King Kong*, there's a scene of people dancing on deck during the *Venture*'s voyage to Skull Island. Christopher Horvath, CG [computer-graphics] supervisor at Weta Digital, views an almost completed shot from the scene on his computer screen. The lively mood of the characters is complemented by a subtle sunset sky, a pleasant breeze, the gentle rocking of the boat, and, in the background, a placidly dancing sea.

The scene was filmed in Studio B against a green screen, so the sea was digitally created and added later. Christopher has been creating water for a decade, but still he's enchanted by the look of these studio-based exterior shots in *King Kong*: "There's nothing extraordinarily complicated about them, but they're really beautiful. I just really like how much they look like they're outside. It's kind of embarrassing that I'm so easily entertained by things that most people in our profession are not supposed to find groundbreaking anymore," he says with a laugh.

Christopher estimates that the number of digital water shots in the movie is approaching four hundred. The problem with real water is that it cannot be directed to perform in particular ways to suit each shot. "Sometimes we're using what we call plate water, which is water

# THE DANCING OCEAN

that was filmed specifically as a backdrop, but then we're intercutting filmed water with CG water."

The software used by the digital water team to create the illusion of ocean waves has been developed with reference to scientific studies of the movement of water. "I'd say we struggle more with light and the interaction of light on the water than we do with the movement," says Christopher. He pulls out a shot of some waves in the early stages of animation. They are simple squiggly lines, like an animated pencil outline of waves. "There have been so many studies, over hundreds of years, about the movement of waves, particularly waves in the deep ocean, because of shipping. There is two hundred years' worth of science as to exactly what the shape of a wake should be. We know exactly how the water should move under certain circumstances." The hard part is filling in the blanks between the squiggles—adding a sealike skin to the dancing wave shapes, refining the surface details, "focusing on making these really simple things very beautiful."

The sunset sequence of Denham doing screen tests of Ann on deck was also shot indoors. "Some of these shots are obviously romanticized—these dreamy, romantic, very idyllic surroundings, twinkling little fairy lights out in the dis-

The live-action shot on the left was composited over with digital ocean and sky, as seen in the image below.

tance. Can you feel that these waves have a bit of a backlit look, like the light is glowing through them a little bit, especially the ones that peak up? Again, it's one of those small, subtle things that we have focused on—just getting that almost translucency. It used to be that just getting the movement right was so hard that the interplay of light and shadow was an afterthought."

Right now, the digital water team is working on the more turbulent sequence in which the *Venture* founders on the rocks off Skull Island. "The boat gets picked up by these big waves and starts getting thrown around," says Christopher. "Now we have this large body of water that's moving much more dramatically than it was before, so there's a whole new issue of water that breaks apart and becomes splashes, then becomes foam and mist. That's our big challenge. . . . We're trying to figure out how to calculate interaction between the water and rocks and how to calculate interaction with the water itself."

Thankfully, well-written software can do some of those calculations for them: "We have something that analyses the surface of the wave and figures out where it's sharp and how hard the wind is pushing against it, and it starts to draw little white lines where it should be starting to break. We don't get to just be artists. I spend most of my time writing software, but with specific artistic goals in mind. I tell my family that we type pictures."

In later shots there are "hero" waves, individual waves that need to perform in a particular way. For those waves, the water team is doing something called wave sculpting: choreographing waves to match the movement of the boat when it's being tossed about in turbulent water. Christopher digs out a previz-style animation of the boat rising on a swell and pivoting in the stormy waves. "This movement will get sent to the miniatures team, which will extract the movement data from these animations and move the miniature boat accordingly. Then they'll film their miniature boat doing that movement. And then we have to sculpt water by hand to match it.

"We spent a couple of months building tools that let us drag water around . . . you have these big arrows, and they're like big steering wheels as to what the wind direction is and what the basic wave direction is, and in this particular case there's a swell here that needed to match the boat being lifted."

The focus is again on detail—getting the waves to move realistically against the boat, with foam and

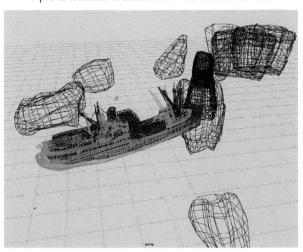

A previz technical breakdown for the miniatures team.

An early water simulation test.

The final shot from the early water simulation test in the previous image.

splashes and tiny capillary waves. "For big waves, the energy that causes the waves to happen comes from the wind, and what brings the waves back down—the restoring force—is gravity. In the case of the little capillary waves, they're so small that the restoring force is the surface tension of the water. They get pushed up into little peaks by the wind, and the surface tension pulls them back. So they have a different look to them. They're more like veins. Our previous challenge was sculpting waves in the first place, but now the challenge is getting the foam and capillary action [right], and getting the splashes to work."

And the next challenge after that? "The sequence in which Kong gets captured has Kong in the water splashing around and hitting boats . . . we have to somehow figure out how to have this CG creature interacting with all this water and making more than just splashes—he's lifting the water because he's so big." You can hear the excitement in Christopher's voice as he anticipates the work ahead.

Conceptual art by Gus Hunter showing sailors desperately trying to escape Kong's fury as he searches for Ann.

Conceptual art by Gus Hunter illustrating the nightmarish design of one side of the log chasm ravine.

"'The moment you step onto Skull Island, it is a horror show.' That initial brief from Peter brought a license to our design that just let us go crazy and create a rich ecosystem," says Weta Workshop's Richard Taylor.

Skull Island is a blend of live-action sets, miniatures, and computer-generated environments, so creating Skull Island has been a collaborative process. The art department has built physical sets with which the actors interact. Weta Workshop has built miniature environments to extend the full-scale sets and to serve as the settings for digital action, such as Kong's battle with the V-Rexes. Weta Digital is creating digital environments and matte paintings to extend beyond the miniatures and into the distance, creating wider vistas and adding details such as sky, waterfalls, and falling rock.

"Everything on Skull Island is intended to be real, but it has to be a little bit bigger than real, a little bit over-the-top," says Alex Funke, director of visual effects photography. "Everything's a little bit bigger, a little bit scarier, a little bit more angular. That's the reason that we're shooting everything either on the back lot, in the studio, or in miniature. If you simply went to a location, you're driven by what the location can give you. Peter wants to give it more."

Hence the wildly overgrown, off-kilter, shattered look to Skull Island: "Everything about the island is completely at odds with humankind, because it is a world that has grown up to the scale of a twenty-five-foot gorilla," says Richard. "Kong can move through the island with ease. A six-foot guy with two legs and a gun can see where he has to go forty feet away, but it may take a day to get there, because he's got to traverse up and down this ecosystem of huge vines and trees. It's not a pleasant Sunday-afternoon romp through the redwoods."

Richard Taylor, production designer Grant Major, and senior visual effects supervisor Joe Letteri all see correlations between Skull Island and the movie's version of New York. "I've always seen them as being very much the same place in some way," says Grant: "the towering buildings of New York and these huge shapes, these big trees, the canyonlike architecture of Skull Island. Getting lost in the complexities of Manhattan, and struggling your way through Skull Island—they have real similarities.

"With the Depression-era view we're showing of New York in the 1930s, and then the abandoned nature of the Skull Island village, there's a direct similarity between the trapped, down and out natives perched on the outside of the island, and the unemployed people that we see in New York.

## SKULL ISLAND

Early illustration concept by Gus Hunter depicting the interior design of Kong's lair, looking out at the island.

"Most graphically, when we're up in Kong's lair, the view out across Skull Island has direct similarities to the view from the top of the Empire State, looking down to lower Manhattan and out to the harbor beyond. When you look at the original movie, they're very similar geographically . . . and symbolically."

Joe Letteri considers the original *King Kong* to be the best touchstone for the design of Skull Island. "You have these incredibly dense, almost film-noirish figures in the foreground, falling off into this hot, steamy, almost bright jungle going into the background. Everywhere you looked there were fantastic creatures lurking. But there was also an otherworldliness to it. It was something that you can't really penetrate.

"Most real jungles have a really thick canopy and things will fall off into darkness as you go off into the distance, with occasional bits of light poking through. But we're adding this steamy, hot element to

it so that, as you look off into the distance, it's kind of bright and you can't really tell what's going on back there. It's dense in an atmospheric way. It almost mimics what we're doing with the coal smoke in New York, but with New York we're keeping it much more realistic. It allows you to do some interesting lighting tricks that can keep the fantasy element a little bit more alive."

"This is a fantasy movie," says Richard, "but, to us, it's imperative that the audience can pin the fantasy of this world into a total reality."

To ensure a richly detailed and cohesive design, a complete history was invented for the lost world. "The audience may never know any of this back history," says Richard, "but unless we, as a group of designers, established it for ourselves, we wouldn't feel equipped to put the architecture, the ancient people, the new people, or the creatures into that world."

Very early concept art by Gus Hunter illustrating the scale of the majestic natural structures that are seen within the jungle interior.

Skull Island ancient architecture concept design by Gus Hunter.

"Skull Island once had a very rich cultural and extravagant populace, on a par with, say, ancient Peruvian culture. The island was a very successful and beautiful trading port. It had a promenade that ran from the main gate down to the sea. There the people traded with the outer islands.

"They had built in a very rich, Indonesian-influenced style. They mined basalt logs—big, hexagonal stems of crystalline rock—from the coastline of the island and utilized those to tie into the architecture of piled rocks. Almost like you can build a twig house, they were able to strap them and tie them together. That gave them the ability, unlike other cultures, to create an ornamental, upswept architectural style to their walls. So their architecture grew to a massive size, because the island had this natural resource. And it grew as a very sophisticated, almost biblical-scale environment.

"The island existed in extreme harmony with its surroundings. The culture of the people had grown up with the knowledge that the island possessed giant gorillas, giant dinosaurs, and an amazing rich and deadly fauna and flora. But they held it at bay with a massive wall that they built around their city, and so controlled their environment. The creatures lived in harmony outside of the wall, the people lived in harmony inside the wall, and everything was in equilibrium.

"But, maybe two thousand years before we enter the story, the seismic eruptions began. Earthquakes began to drop the wall. Slices of the island began to fall away. In fact, the whole island began to sink. That created social chaos within the infrastructure of the city. But also, the wall began to crumble, allowing the creatures into the inner sanctum of the village. Chaos reigned and the people were wiped out. Whether there was infighting, starvation, or they were killed off by these huge predators, we have no idea, but that's ultimately what happened.

"Our natives arrived maybe four generations before we do in 1933 and found the remains of this culture. By now the whole island was distressed and collapsed. Most of the island had sunk. Most of the wall, indeed most of this beautiful island, had gone. The creatures hadn't fallen into the ocean, of course. They had just condensed and moved in. There was one last remaining tiny piece of wall.

"The natives, haplessly blown off course by the winds of the Indonesian oceans, have landed on this desolate, windblown, sea-salt-swept outcrop of

# A BRIEF HISTORY OF SKULL ISLAND

AS TOLD BY RICHARD TAYLOR

Top: Wide concept by Gus Hunter of the village and fiery wall during Ann's sacrifice to Kong.
Bottom: Concept art by Gus Hunter depicting *Venture* crewmen rowing through a maze of eroded,
ghoulish pinnacle structures as they approach Skull Island.

rock, outside the wall, and there they have to live. There they have to survive. All of their previous culture, the harmony that they had in their previous life and the sophistication of their seafaring, is stripped away, due to basic survival instinct. Their weapons pay no homage to their ancient culture—they're utilitarian, for fishing, hunting, and survival. At best they can fish or hunt seabirds. Beyond the wall, it's rich, lush, full of beautiful food sources, but it's dangerous. Over the wall are the creatures that hold them at bay. So their whole life they stay clinging to this tiny outcrop of rock. Their sole purpose is survival.

"They have no ceremony about them, other than their sacrificial offering to Kong. Every six or twelve months they're sacrificing yet another young woman to appease him, and the gene pool is further deteriorating, causing more and more aggression in the males, because there are less and less women. The feudal system within the culture of the village is so dramatic and so aggressive that they are slowly depopulating and undermining their own survival. They're barely clinging to existence. If we had arrived on the island another sixty years [after] 1933, there's a bloody good chance that they would have died out.

"Our sailors arrive on the island through an underground cave—or so they think. It is actually a massive amphitheater, carved into the solid rock with burial chambers for the gentry of the ancient city. The chamber has split in half and sunk into the ocean. The stairs to the burial chambers are now on a tilt. As the sailors climb up to the point where they pop out in front of the wall, they're actually walking through the old crypts that have been long since stripped of any of their corpses, because the natives, in desperate need of habitation, have pulled the corpses out and now live in the crypts themselves, in amongst the remnants of these ancient people.

"What the sailors discover when they venture across the wall is a saturated ecosystem of creatures. Everywhere you look there are lizards, insects, snails, deadly plants . . . dinosaurs, swamp creatures, and bats. It's all condensed down into this ecosystem unlike anywhere else in the world.

"The city is now totally grown over with dense jungle. But still coming through that are massive architectural structures. The brontosaurs stampede down the boulevard of a massive central city promenade. Eventually, the last remnant of wall is going to fall into the ocean. And, ultimately, what now remains of the island will go with it."

Sam Manzanza, ready for filming.

A photograph in *National Geographic* magazine leapt out at Peter Jackson as having something of the look he wanted for the Skull Island inhabitants. It was a portrait of a man with ultradark skin and bright red eyes. The image was unsettling—just as Peter wanted the Skull Islanders to be.

The islanders are the savage remnants of a displaced tribal group, struggling to survive on a barren outcrop of coastal rock. "They have no ability to adorn their costuming with anything more than shreddings of crude flax, the backbones of fish, and sea urchin spines," says Richard Taylor. "The most high-ranking people in the village get to use the feathers that have fallen from birds. But for the most part, their adornment is extremely crude. Everything is dank and black and oily. They have no ability to stay clean or dry or colorful. There are no pigments in the rock, they can't mine for oxides, so they've got no ability to bring color to their lives. They wouldn't even want to anymore."

They can, however, stick bones through their skin, chip their teeth, and turn the whites of their eyes red. "Peter wanted these natives to be really aggressive," says prosthetics supervisor Gino Acevedo. "They're not afraid of pain."

One hundred actors and extras played the Skull Islanders. Rather than skewer

# THE PEOPLE OF SKULL ISLAND

their skin with shards of bone, the prosthetics team at Weta Workshop made them fake noses and bumps of raised skin out of foam rubber. The bits of bone and wood piercing the prosthetic pieces look sharp, but for safety reasons are actually quite soft and flexible, cast out of a soft urethane and painted accordingly.

The man in the *National Geographic* photograph was from an African tribe with a tradition of squirting juice from a certain berry into their eyes on ceremonial occasions, causing the whites of the eyes to turn red. The prosthetics team opted instead to make reddish sclera lenses, which cover the entire front of the eye. Sclera lenses were also used to create the illusion of cataracts, and for the drummers who appear to go into a trance and roll their eyes back into their head.

Dentures were made to give the impression of broken teeth. "There are some tribes that actually file their teeth to a point," says Gino, "but Peter said, 'No, no, I want them to look as if they got a sharp instrument and a rock and went clunk, and chipped the tooth.'"

Dental alginate was used to take a mold of each actor's real teeth, and plaster was poured into the mold to create an exact duplicate of the teeth. Sculptors then added modeling clay to each plaster tooth

Weta Workshop's Greg Tozer puts finishing touches to a Skull Islander wig.

and sculpted suitably broken edges. Then the molding and plastering routine was repeated to get a hard copy of the broken teeth. "We've got a vacuform machine, which heats up a really thin sheet of clear plastic, very soft and pliable, and it uses a vacuum to pull the plastic down over the teeth," says Gino. "It cools off right away, and then we can trim it off following the gum line, paint it with special paint, and we have a new set of custom-fit dentures the actors can pop over their own teeth."

Dreadlock wigs were made with a combination of human and yak hair, hand-knotted one hair at a time. It took four months for a team of wigmakers to knot all the wigs.

Actress Vicky Haughton needed to be aged considerably to play the old sha-woman who adorns Ann with a necklace as part of the sacrificial ritual. "Peter wanted her to be icky-looking, really weathered," says Gino. "We did a makeup test on her without prosthetics, using a process known as old-age stipple. You stretch the skin, stipple on about three layers of liquid latex, let each layer dry in between, and then you powder it, and when you release it, it forms all these natural wrinkles. Unfortunately for us, her skin was

just too good and healthy. The wrinkles just didn't show up. So I gave Peter an option that we could use prosthetics to really change her features—including her hands. I wanted to make her knuckles arthritic—really twisted and bony."

The facial prosthetics completely encased Vicky's head. Her hair was smoothed away under a bald cap, then the prosthetics went on in pieces—first the neck piece, then the facial piece, a forehead piece, and a piece for the back of the head, each one overlapping at the edges. "We do it in pieces because it makes it easier for us to glue it all down," Gino explains. "If you have areas that are loose, it really shows up when she starts moving her face and you get a kind of weird buckling." It took five hours to complete Vicky's makeup each day.

Vicky's prosthetic pieces were made out of velvety soft, squishy silicone, which is more expensive than the foam rubber used for most of the pros-

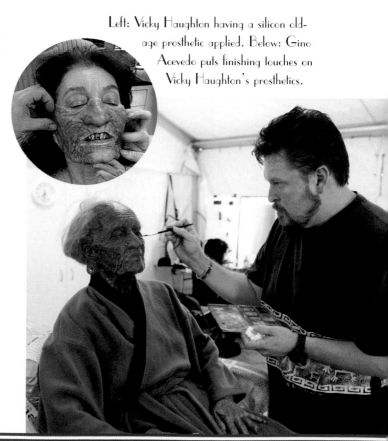

Left: Vicky Haughton having a silicon old-age prosthetic applied. Below: Gino Acevedo puts finishing touches on Vicky Haughton's prosthetics.

thetic noses, but has the translucency and mobility of skin. "It was all very soft for her so that when she made expressions, it would come through the appliances—you could still read her face," says Gino.

"I love doing the first makeup test on the actors. Vicky started really getting into the character. Usually what I like to do after you've put them into the makeup is to leave the actor alone for a few minutes in front of the mirror, so they can really get used to their new layer of skin. They're so used to their faces when they're acting, but if their expressions are too subtle, they won't read through the prosthetic. So they have to really get in there and move their face

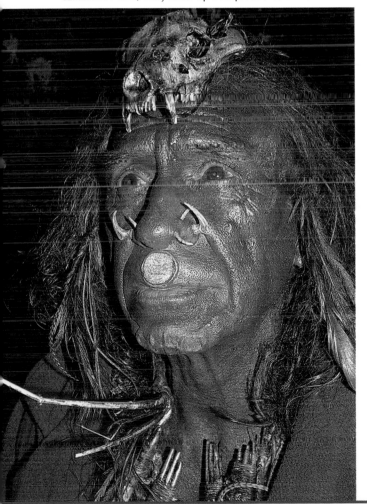

Tamihana Nuku, fully made up with prosthetics and contacts.

around and see what it looks like and what they can do with it."

The actors and extras playing the islanders are a mixture of races—some African, others Maori, Polynesian, or Asian. They were all spray-painted to make their skin darker. "Peter really liked the color of the Sudanese people," says Gino. "They have the most beautiful black skin. It's almost purple."

Getting into full-body makeup required the actors to set aside any sense of modesty. "We had these big spray guns like they use to spray cars, but we put our special makeup paint in there. The actors undressed all the way down to a G-string, and they had to do a spread-eagle pose and our guys would spray their fronts and backs."

The native village and wall set, too big to build in a soundstage, was erected outside on nearby Mount Crawford, a hill overlooking Wellington harbor. There were no permanent facilities there, so marquees were set up as changing rooms, spray booths, drying rooms, and shower blocks. It took several hours to get one hundred Skull Islanders painted, dried, scarred, pierced, wigged, scantily clad, and ready for a wet night of drumming or skulking.

Afterward, it took a good forty-five minutes of vigorous scrubbing for each Skull Islander to get clean, because the body makeup was alcohol-based so that it wouldn't wash off when the special effects team turned on the rain. "We gave them 'welcome packs' with big bottles of all the different products they needed," says Jamie Wilson, Weta Workshop's on-set coordinator. "You had to be pretty hands-on, and everyone was helping each other out, because that paint sticks like nobody's business."

Putting on the makeup and prosthetics was not all it took to transform the actors and extras into Skull Islanders. They also had to learn the unique cultural behavior of the tribe. "They had performance coaches, and they had a dance coach," says

Skull Islanders rehearse their moves.

Jamie. "They did five days of rehearsals in a gym hall to start off with—rehearsing with the weapons, doing the drumming, and getting the emotive feel to the performance, and also bonding as a group, because on the whole nobody had met anybody else. You had to get people used to being with each other, and you had the hurdle of a certain element of naked-ness, so there was an element of exposing yourself to a whole lot of other people you'd never met before."

A team of three or four model-makers spent three weeks making spears and clubs for the Skull Islanders. Many of the weapons were quickly assembled from a vicious-looking collection of plastic bones, bird beaks, shark teeth, and tiny skulls, tied onto bits of bamboo or roughed-up dowels with tarred marline or cloth. "They're desperate people hanging on to what's left of their lives and their island," says Weta Work-shop supervisor Jason Docherty. "Their costumes are crude, they're crude, their weapons are crude."

Although the weapons seem barbaric, most are harmless. Spearheads that look like razor-sharp flint were fashioned out of soft rubber. Savage-looking clubs were molded from plastic. Any weapon to be wielded against an actor, as opposed to simply car-ried or brandished, was made from softer, more flexi-ble urethane.

A line-up of Skull Islander weapons.

112

Denham's sound recordist comes to a grisly end, skewered by a spear, so a special spear rig was made for the actor playing the role. "We took a cast of his torso," says Jason, "and then we used a fiberglass product called Kevlar, which is used to make bulletproof vests—it's very strong and light. We made a Kevlar shell, and it's got a couple of little anchoring points front and back, and you chop the spear, and the little front bit plugs in and the little back bit plugs in. And then they'll do a shot with him running, they'll do a shot with the native throwing the spear, and they'll do a shot with him stopping and he's got the front sticking out, and he falls over and he's finished. Just to get that shot, we've had to make about five repeats of the spear.

If there's a possibility it could break, we make multiple reproductions."

It took twelve or thirteen days to film the Skull Islander scenes, mostly at night. "It definitely wasn't for the shy or fainthearted," says Jamie Wilson. "Most of the time on set was spent under rain towers, and it was cold, so we had lots of blankets, dressing gowns, hot-water bottles, hot drinks, and refreshments to keep them going.

"All these people went out, day after day, knowing what was coming—and the shiver that went down the spine when those first drops of water came, freezing cold, out of the rain tower above them! We thought we'd do day one and nobody would want to come back, but they were troopers."

A wide shot of the wall set, representing the bottom third of the wall. The upper two-thirds was built in miniature.

Skull Island is somewhere off the coast of Sumatra, where tectonic plates collide. It is a dangerous place. Its dense jungle is teeming with poisonous things, sharp things, things that bite. Its brutal landscape, forged by violent volcanic eruptions, has been shattered by earthquakes. The island is breaking apart.

An aggressive landscape required the building of aggressive sets, says supervising art director Dan Hennah. "Everywhere you look, you'd expect to see great fissures and cracks, an undercut cliff or a piece of flat land tilted over, a bit of road angling off towards a cliff edge—vertigo-inducing stuff. We're all the time trying to say that the reason no one's found this island is that maybe the whole thing has sunk into the sea. Back in 1933 it was on the way, but maybe now it's gone."

The great wall that once surrounded an ancient city is one of the first indicators of the destructive forces at work on Skull Island. Broken segments of wall tilting into the sea were built as miniatures by Weta Workshop. The art department, meanwhile, built the native village and an enormous section of the wall, including the gates to the overgrown city, on Mount Crawford, just ten minutes' drive from Stone Street Studios.

Although not as large as the New York set, the wall and village set was a huge undertaking, constructed over two acres. The set was designed to establish two layers of culture—the flimsy bamboo culture of the current inhabitants and the monumental legacy of an extinct civilization. A dramatic landscape of rock and fissures was roughed out in wooden geometric shapes by the construction department, then clad with polystyrene and concrete. Only the bottom third of the wall was built as a set, with the upper two-thirds being built in miniature. Even so, the wall stood twelve meters high (almost forty feet).

## BIG ROCKS AND TREES

"It was a brilliant set—that huge wall was just astounding," says actor Jed Brophy. "When you were going through those huge gates, it wasn't hard to manufacture the feeling of awe and fear because it *was* awesome."

The very top of the wall above the gates was built as a separate set in Studio X. It was seven meters high and included a wall-top walkway and part of the contraption used to sacrifice Ann to Kong. Another set, four meters high, consisted simply of poles on which the native drummers perched high above the wall. The altar, where Kong snatches Ann, was built as a separate set again in Studio Q.

Steve Ingram's special effects team created wind, smoke, and fire for the wall-top scenes. "At the top of the wall we had some in situ propane flames," he says. "We

Top: Interior set of the sacrificial altar. Below: An interior jungle set.

Top: An example of Skull Island architecture. Below: Drystone walling built from spray foam and polystyrene.

had the ability to make them fairly huge, but they wanted the villagers all around the wall—enough in the shot that you couldn't have the flames turned up too high because they were too hot and too close. The natives light some burning liquid, the liquid flows down troughs, then it cuts to the big wall shot with the skull all in flames. In the wide shot it's all digital, but with the natives in the close shots and midshots, that's all real. We made up a mix that was flammable, but not too volatile, that we could pump out of pressure pots. They could light it, then we'd slowly bring the pressure up to create these flowing rivers of flame."

The bridge contraption that delivers Ann to the sacrificial altar was built in two parts: the top part on rollers to initiate the move away from the wall, and a more complete rig to bring her down onto the altar. "It looks like a bamboo structure, but inside it's steel," says construction supervisor Ed Mulholland. "If you're hanging a million-dollar actor off it, it's got to be secure and safe. The closer you get to the actors, the safer things have to be."

Another impressive set was a section of stone pathway and wall, part of the gorge where Denham

and the crew are trampled by a herd of Brontosaurs. It was built at Windy Point on the south coast where there was enough room for the actors to build up some speed to run at full tilt and imagine being chased by dinosaurs. "Peter said, 'You look up to the left and there's a foot, and you look to the right and there's a foot,' so he gave us a pretty good map to where feet were coming down so we were all looking in the right place," says Jed Brophy. "But it took a few takes to get it. It was just a matter of getting in your head that you are terrified and that you're running for your life, but also being able to run and turn around and look at whatever's coming behind you without falling flat on your face. We were running down big stone steps, and that was pretty tricky, because if you missed your footing . . . Someone did fall over at one stage."

For the sculpture department, tasked with fabricating all the rocklike surfaces for the Skull Island sets, the Mount Crawford and Windy Point sets were quite an achievement, according to sculpture supervisor Ra Vincent. Ra's team, numbering sometimes as many as forty carvers, spent months making rock, including the boulders and paving

Simon Harper, 2nd unit on-set art director, setting up Carl Denham's Bell & Howell camera prop at the Brontosaur stampede set.

Bottom of the log chasm's interior studio set, dressed with dinosaur bones.

stones that make up walls, doorways, and roads, the great carved-face statues, and the rocky texture of the jagged landscape. "The wall was a massive build, but the village in front of it was just as massive," he says.

Skull Island's lost civilization built a gigantic drystone wall anchored by huge columns of natural basalt. Ra's team fashioned boulders and basalt out of spray foam and polystyrene. For the drystone walling, they made thirty-eight panels of boulders, four meters wide and two and a half meters high, with twenty to twenty-five rocks per panel. The panels were then lifted by crane and fixed to scaffolding towers. "Once all the rock panels were on, the scaffolders put up a good working platform all the way around, and we all got up there in our harnesses and made little individual rocks to put in between all the seams."

Polystyrene was also used to texture the landscape in front of the wall. The carvers used chain saws, hot wires, heat guns, angle-grinders, and knives. "Angle-grinding polystyrene, that's one of my favorites," says Ra, "but the Tajima, the biggest snap-blade knife you can buy, is our number one tool. All

our edges had to be supercrisp—nice hard edges, glassy, basalt, lava. They wanted a hard volcanic look, so everything was pointy and nasty. A technique we used . . . for sculpting rocks was to do slight scalloped cuts, which meant that all the high points on your stones had a very sharp edge."

Surfaces intended for heavy foot traffic were strengthened with a layer of concrete, and industrial tinfoil, scrunched up and pressed into the wet cement, gave the concrete a rocky texture. The carvers also used latex molds. Says Ra, "When you wanted a really nice piece, you put a mold of a real rock into the wet cement. Quite often, the following day we'd come back with small barrow loads of cement and make special little bits, because, in the fervor and mayhem of emptying tons and tons of concrete, you can't get too artistic."

To safeguard the actors and stunt performers in action areas, softer rock surfaces were made from rubber sprayed into the molds of real rock. Selected rock faces on Wellington's craggy shoreline were replicated and used many times over. The sculptors scouted for rock faces with just the right qualities. "There was one in Breaker Bay right out on the end of the point," says Ra. "The mold-maker had to walk four hundred meters down the beach with huge pails of silicone and generators and heaters and spend a couple of days out there taking texture stamps off the natural rock walls."

Once sculpted, the rock surfaces were plastered and painted by the set finishers, and the greens department added lichens, gravel, and grit. Set dressers scattered broken shells and burnt wood, erected the bamboo structures of the latter-day natives, and decorated the set with skulls and corpses.

The gruesome job of making and mangling human remains for the set fell to Weta Workshop. About forty generic body shapes were cast in urethane from two different molds, then chopped and

Life-size skull of Kong's father.

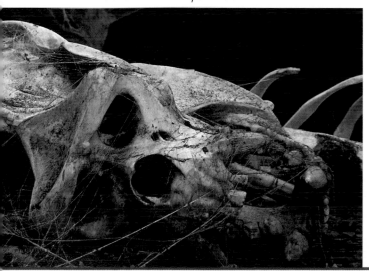

119

changed for individualized looks, says workshop supervisor Jason Docherty: "You just cut the head off, turn the head, cut the arm off, change the orientation of the arm, and put latex and tissue all over it to give it this mummified look."

Weta Workshop also provided skeletons, skulls, and bones for other Skull Island sets, including a hundred bodies' worth of human bones for the bone fields where the remains of Kong's past sacrificial victims lie. "They're cheap plastic skeletons," reveals Jason. "A human body has two hundred and something bones, so to mold a human skeleton costs thousands of dollars. You can buy full Halloween skeletons, unassembled, from a commercial company in America that has them made in China and they're only one hundred dollars each. We dolled them all up. We just did it one weekend. In some cases we made them look like they've got a little bit of meat on them, and then we painted them up for the bone fields."

Weta Workshop also made jumbo-size bones for Kong's lair, a studio set. They represent the skeleton of Kong's father or mother, suggesting he once had a family and has not always been a solitary creature. The props makers stuck hair and latex to the bones to make it look as though the animal's fur is still rotting away.

The set dressers decorated that part of the lair with spiderwebs made from "some horrible toxic stuff that they put into padded bras," says Tanea Chapman, supervising set dresser. "You heat it up to a really hot temperature and put it in a cobweb-spinning gun on the end of a drill. It spits out in a circle and laces itself and looks like a spiderweb. You can stretch it and you can wrap things in it. It's fantastic."

Most of the jungle sets were built in New Zealand's largest soundstage, the brand-new Kong Stage, constructed at Stone Street Studios just in time for filming. In fact, the roof was going onto the soundstage as the set for the killing ground, where

Kong disposes of his victims, was being built inside. The Stone Street Studios complex was once a gas-works and later a paint factory, so many of the studios and workshops are converted warehouses. Kong Stage is a purpose-built soundstage, 24,500 square feet in area and forty feet high—room for plenty of trees, rocks, and big background blue screens.

The art department was undaunted by the prospect of building a jungle, having developed considerable expertise on *The Lord of the Rings.* "We'd worked on Fangorn Forest and established a whole lot of techniques for building forests," says Dan Hennah. "A jungle's got a lot of very similar elements—big trees, lots of foliage." The brief for Skull Island was to create a fantastical yet realistic-looking jungle, so the sets include both real and man-made plants and trees.

Out back, behind the stages, the art department built four greenhouses and a couple of shade houses for a jungle-style nursery. They spent six months researching jungle flora and shopping for plants in forests, nurseries, and farms throughout New Zealand, then filled the greenhouses with live tree ferns, climbers, grasses, mosses, and all manner of slightly unusual plants.

With Jack Driscoll, Carl Denham, and the sailors trekking all through the jungle in search of Ann, many different jungle sets were required. The greens team, at times as many as fifty people, has been kept frantically busy rearranging greenery. "They film for a couple of days, or a day," says greens foreman Simon Lowe, "and then we have a night shift come in and completely change the set to a swamp, or remove foliage, or just try and change the look. So the sets are constantly revolving and changing, which is great for the film crew, but very taxing for us."

121

Top: Vines made out of soft rubber. Below: Production designer Grant Major directing construction at the Skull Island swamp set on the backlot at Stone Street Studios.

Taxing for the greenery too—studio lighting takes its toll on live foliage. The greens team lavishes care and attention on the plants, keeping them constantly damp, sending them back to the nursery when they start to droop, and replenishing the sets with fresh foliage every couple of days. But after two or three stints on set, plants such as mosses start to look a bit sad, says Simon. "So then we can break them up and use them as forest litter on the forest floor or in ruts and dark places where you have a lot of organic matter building up."

Nestled among the live flora on the jungle sets is a huge variety of artificial plants, from big trees to small lichens. "If you have a big studio like Kong Stage, trying to fill that with real greens would be an ecological disaster. To have a balance of artificial and real is the key. If you have it all artificial, it really stands out, but if you have a few real elements amongst it, it sells it." For example, moss seen in the foreground of a shot is likely to be real, bought from moss farms; in the background, a carpet of moss-colored, slightly singed fake fur looks indistinguishable from the live moss.

Two containerloads of artificial plants and flowers were shipped in from China, but many plants have been made on-site by the art department. A special prehistoric department was set up to develop the more oddball flowers and plants, says Dan Hennah. "We've had three to five people working for almost a year, making upside-down flowers and insect-eating plants, largely based on historical research into now extinct plants from the dinosaur era, but also some slightly fanciful variations—great big spongy, slippery flowers."

Overhead shot of the swamp set.

122

Vines can be made out of foam: "Just like your bed-mattress foam, but in cords, just dipped through latex baths," says Simon. "We also burnt and textured a lot of rope, trying to add some interest to it—you get a bit of a gnarly effect with it. We made up a series of sections of vines using a mold, and that worked quite well for the larger vines. They're a soft rubber and they have a texture of pohutukawa bark on them. And we've used a lot of native supplejack as well."

And then there are the big trees—as many as fifty or sixty for one piece of jungle. They needed to be lightweight, easy to maneuver, premade, and ready to be swung into position at a moment's notice. Glancing around the Stone Street Studios lot, one might be forgiven for thinking someone has run amok with a chain saw. The fences and exterior walls are lined with fallen tree trunks. Closer in-

spection reveals that they are made of polystyrene.

"If the tree is not too complicated with shapes and sizes, we use polystyrene," says Simon. "If we start getting a lot of limbs and laterals and a lot of weight on them, we build a steel structure and clad it in polystyrene. You've got to get the engineering and counterbalancing right before you start cladding."

Building a single tree involves several different teams within the art department. The engineers build the steel armature; the carvers sculpt the polystyrene; the mold-maker makes molds of real bark; the set finishers plaster over the polystyrene, use the molds to stamp an imprint of bark texture into the plaster, then paint the tree; the greens team dresses it with leaves and vines. For more detailed bark textures, many tree trunks are wrapped in rubber bark, from molds taken off macrocarpa or pohutukawa trees. Taller trees tend

123

Peter Jackson walks along Skull Island's rocky shore.

124

Climbing among fake trees on an interior jungle set.

not to require a canopy of leaves. Their trunks end abruptly as if the upper trunk and branches have been sawn off, and the foliage will be created by Weta Digital. Those that do require leaves have the tips of real branches grafted onto them and sprays of plastic and silk foliage attached by hand. "One tree might end up with twelve thousand sprays on it, depending on the size of the tree," says Simon, "and they're all individually put on."

The hollow log in which Ann seeks refuge from some hungry carnivores was ten meters (almost thirty-three feet) long and two meters (six and a half feet) in diameter. The biggest upright trees were six meters (nineteen and a half feet) high and about ten meters in diameter at ground level. "They were rising up out of the water of the swamp," says Dan. "In terms of the degree of difficulty, they were the hard-

est. They had to be light enough for us to move around, but not so light that they floated in the swamp. So they've got concrete in the bottom, not too much foam."

A swamp was created outside on a patch of parking lot doubling as a back lot at Stone Street Studios. A rim for the wet set was built up using wire baskets packed with rocks, and the set was then filled with 1.8 million liters (nearly five hundred thousand gallons) of water. The set finishers colored the water with food dye and made pond scum to float on the surface. "We used beaded polystyrene just ground off a polystyrene block," says set finishing supervisor Kathryn Lim, "and we colored that in a concrete mixer with paint and then, when it was dry, chucked it in the pool."

Coming up with recipes for such unlikely items as pond scum typically involves expertise, trial and error, and sometimes a little bit of serendipity. Wax beads and bean-bag balls were used for earlier attempts at making pond scum, but they looked too symmetrical. Grinding the polystyrene produced beads of different sizes. "When you broke down the beads, there was this kind of weird, kinetic, magnetic thing going on with the scum, so they clung to each other. So, when the boat went through the water, the pond scum parted and then it closed in again behind. It turned out really well."

A patch of Skull Island's rocky shore was also built as a wet set. The greens team obtained consent to collect seaweed washed up around Wellington's coastlines for the set. Set dressers scattered seashells and glued fake limpets to the rocks. "The props makers made these lovely little anemones, and the guys glued them just under the waterline before they filled the water up," says supervising set dresser Tanea Chapman. "When you looked in rock pools, you saw these little jellied anemones." Not that audiences are likely to look that close: "You'll never see any of it," she says with a rueful laugh.

Even mud has been specially made for the Skull Island sets. Typical ingredients for hygienic, colorfast mud are sterilized peat and wallpaper paste. A ready supply of waste sawdust from the construction department provides the raw material for a variety of other set finishings. "We've spent hours and hours on sawdust . . . because they'd want tiny little bits of dirt and larger pieces of peat and things like that," says Kathryn. "We'll mix sawdust, plaster, and paint and just throw it at the set. It just splats on and looks like moss or lichen."

In one of the most memorable scenes from the 1933 version of *King Kong*, Kong shakes the *Venture* search party off a huge log spanning a deep ravine. The sequence was an extraordinary special effects achievement for its time, combining the stop-motion Kong puppet and a miniature tree trunk with footage

of the actors walking up and falling off an unseen ramp. In Peter Jackson's *King Kong*, the actors were able to fall off the log itself, but the log was built in three separate pieces.

The log chasm set, in Kong Stage, consisted of the two opposite edges of the chasm, but not the chasm itself, which would be built as a miniature. Each side of the chasm sported one end of the log—a fallen tree—with the middle of the log missing. The chasm on set was just one meter deep on one side and two meters on the other, so the actors were able to emerge from the jungle, walk along the edge of the ravine, and step onto the log on one side of the set, and later step off the log on the other side of the set.

All the action on the fallen trunk was filmed in Stage A against blue screens. The missing middle section of the trunk was built on a computer-controlled motion rig so its movement could be programmed to match the actions of the digital Kong. The log was made of polystyrene with a steel frame running through it, soft rubber bark, and safety mats on the floor beneath it. Anchor points were built into the log so that the actors and stunt performers could be harnessed to it if necessary. For the most violent movements, stuntmen stood in for the actors. The actors were swapped in for close-ups of their characters clinging to the bucking log for dear life.

The log marked the end of the road for Jed Brophy's character, Skeggs, who survived such dangers as the swamp and the Brontosaur stampede only to plunge to a sticky fate at the log chasm. "I died a very innocuous death when I just fell to my death in the pit. I would have loved it to have been a bit more gruesome." Jed laughs. "The log was a big hydraulic thing and it lifted up and down and we just fell off it onto a mat. And that was the end of me as far as I know. Once I'm dead, I get eaten by a giant slug, I'm told, but I haven't seen the slug, so I couldn't tell you."

Miniature (1:12 scale) altar set.

"On *The Lord of the Rings*, we built seventy-two miniatures in five and a half years, which we thought was fast enough," says Richard Taylor, head of Weta Workshop. "For *King Kong* we have to build forty-two miniatures in just over a year, so we have to deliver a miniature every week and a half to the shooting stage."

We are standing sandwiched between two rocky cliffs that are anything but miniature. They rise up to the ceiling grid and run the length of Weta Workshop's cavernous miniatures studio. "We call our miniatures 'bigatures,'" Richard says with a grin. "This one is the log chasm."

In some ways, building miniature rock is exactly the same as building big rock for the live-action sets—including the use of textured surfaces cast from molds taken from real rock. Richard spreads his hand against a molded section of the chasm: "The wonderful thing about rock is that it has no scale. I could be putting my hand on a piece of rock as I clamber across the coastline of Wellington—or you could composite a climber that is only three millimeters tall onto this ledge and he would look like he's climbing a mountain."

Up near the ceiling, sculptors clamber over the miniature, hacking at the fake rock with their carving knives, scrabbling bits away with their fingers. Even at flesh-and-blood human scale, they still look like

# LITTLE ROCKS AND TREES

mountaineers on the immense structure.

High up on one precipice a three-foot log juts out into midair. Perched on the log is a little cardboard cutout person, just six inches tall. This towering minichasm is one-tenth of the size it will be to Ann's rescue party in the movie, and this is just half of it. Richard says, "In reality, this would be much deeper than it is at the moment, and that's the next miniature that the team is starting on—the remainder of the chasm and the pit below where they all fall."

This part of the chasm will be on the miniatures stage by next week. "Everything we build has to go through the doors, and then onto house transporters," says Richard. In this case, several house transporters.

Six weeks later, the log chasm barely registers as a distant memory. The pace of work was swift and efficient then, but now there are two miniatures units to feed—a second unit has sprung into being and Weta Workshop is now supplying miniatures for two crews filming on eight separate shooting stages. To add to the challenge, extra miniatures are unexpectedly needed for shots for the movie's publicity trailer.

"Stuff that we never thought was needed for a long time, now is needed within the next week and a half," says Richard. "I don't think we've ever delivered so much product in such a short length of time. We've reallocated people from other parts of the facility into miniatures. Big training camps! But for them it's exciting, we're meeting our deadlines, and Peter likes what we're producing. It's exhilarating!"

Standing majestically at one end of the miniatures studio, Kong's lair is awaiting finishing touches. It is on the back burner for now—more urgent tasks have jumped the line. Behind the lair, an entire wall of enormous shelves is jam-packed with design maquettes, the smaller-scale study models used in the design process—dozens of vignettes reflecting the broken, collapsing, uplifted landscape of shattered rock that is Skull Island.

"All the creative work on the miniatures is done in small scale, usually by the conceptual artists and a few key people," explains miniatures supervisor John Baster. "When an environment is designed, Peter will lock off on certain illustrations that he likes. We take that brief, build a small plasticine maquette, and take it back to Peter. If he doesn't like it, those early little studies are often chopped up with a Stanley knife and rearranged right there in the meeting.

"Once we get that little maquette right, we build a bigger one. We jump up from something you can hold in your hand to something that's table-sized. We do all the details—everything is worked out on that model. Once Peter has approved that, we reproduce it as a full miniature, about ten times bigger."

To replicate the maquette, the miniatures team slices it into a series of profiles. John says, "We put it through a huge band saw, then we very carefully place all the pieces back together before we forget where they go. Then we slip pieces of cardboard in between the cuts and draw around the shapes, so we can plot it all out on five-meter blocks of polystyrene.

"It's like model railways—when you build your railway landscape, you make an egg crate out of cardboard and you slot it all together and cover it with papier-mâché. Well, we make a massive egg crate out of polystyrene with vertical ribs and big polystyrene knobs, and we create this big three-dimensional skeleton—same way as if you built a boat with ribs. It's a simple way of getting the shape. And then on that we hang our skin—our detailed rock faces or landscape items."

The far end of the cavernous studio is bustling with activity. Above the noise of band saws, ventilation equipment, and upbeat music, voices shout directions and advice as sculptors swarm over a huge structure of white polystyrene. Inside the structure is a deep cave with rocky walls.

"This is the sea cave where the *Venture* crew rows ashore," says John. "They land on this rocky outcrop and then go up a series of stairs to the interior of the island. This is radically different from the original artwork. Peter came and looked at it for five minutes

Richard Taylor and Peter Jackson consult on the placement of miniatures while Jeremy Bennett looks on.

John Baster, Ian Ruxton, and Dan Bennett working on a miniature.

and said, 'It would be really cool if this whole thing had fallen down and jammed itself together in a rock pile over this entrance.'"

We crawl under an overhang of cascading polyurethane rock and squat inside the cave. It creaks, squeaks, and shakes as the model-makers work overhead. Unfazed, John calmly points out a set of tiny stairs climbing into a long tunnel. "That bit of miniature there, the stairway, has been perfectly copied from the full-size set that the art department built."

The cave shudders as someone up top starts sawing into the polystyrene. "We've made it so it's nice and strong," says John reassuringly. "You could cut a lot of it away and it would still support itself. There's no timber or steel in the structure, so it's really easy for the team down at the shooting stage to just cut a hole to adapt it to their needs. The whole thing is split down the middle, so they can take the whole side off, or they could cut the roof off and bring the camera down through the top."

Someone drags up a length of wood to brace the cave entrance, while others push and shove at a polystyrene post, driving it into the back of the facade. The cave lurches. "This large overhanging facade looks very threatening, and in actual fact does really want to tip over and land on us," says John, "so we want to make sure it's got a good foundation."

Nearby, there's a strange arrangement of polystyrene pillars sticking up from another sheet of polystyrene like a bizarre multilegged, upside-down table. On top of each pillar is a painted rock. Each is precisely positioned to match animation of Kong as he chases Denham and crew into the sea. "Inside the cave, there are a whole lot of rocks in the water that have to be just the right shape and in just the right place for Kong to be able to stand on them," John explains.

He leads the way to a tabletop maquette. It shows a coastal cove, with tiny stairs through a small cave at one side leading to a rickety stick bridge across a ravine and into a cavern lined with man-made architecture. Fully painted and beautifully detailed, it is soon to be sliced into cross-sections in preparation for the next build. "The sea is surging through here," explains John. "You'll get the feeling that the whole island is really unstable—it's breaking apart and splitting. Even under your feet you can feel the ground vibrating from the waves smashing under your feet. And in this void, it's the first big reveal when suddenly there's an ancient city.

"There's a lot of digital animation which has to take place on the miniature environments. Kong climbs down here and interacts with a lot of the surface, so we're going to have to get computer printouts of the previz environment. Wherever Kong is touch-

129

Miniature (1:12 scale) cathedral cove set.

John Baster, Greg Tozer, and Rob Gillies working on a wall miniature.

Working on a miniature for the Brontosaur stampede sequence.

human beings working with rulers and craft knives. It's not a precise science. We do our best work when we're working fairly freely and have an element of creative freedom," says John. "It's been quite a challenge to incorporate the red-carpet precision into our building process."

Slap-bang in the middle of the studio, model-maker Gareth McGhie is assembling a miniature of the whole of Skull Island. Peter Jackson has planned a shot that will push in low toward the seawall in the foreground, then lift to reveal a series of background mountain ranges.

"This one is a different model," says Gareth. "It's a stand-alone build, not based off anything that has [been] shot as a live scenario. It's a freehand sculpt based on artwork that is from a forced perspective. The foreground, where this wall is arcing into the sea, is at a 1 to 100 scale. The background elements are something like 1 to 1,000. If we were actually building it all at 1 to 100 scale, the hills in the background would be something like a thousand feet tall."

The four-layer background of mountain ranges has been built in four separate pieces. "When you line them up, sit one behind the other, you end up with this great vista of the entire island," says Gareth. "They'll push fog in from both sides, and we're painting the back layers in lighter colors to help give a sense of depth."

In the foreground, Gareth has positioned some broken sections of the wall where the *Venture* will founder. "The boat makes this bit of wall look about a hundred feet tall. In reality it's about one foot!" He laughs. "When you look through the camera, it blows your mind. When you look at your miniature with your eyes, you automatically take in what's at the sides and the workshop lighting, but when you look through the lens—wow! It's a whole new world."

A larger-scale section of wall is out in the paint shop waiting to be painted. It looks as if it has been

ing the rock and wherever people are running, we'll base it on the previz, and where no one is touching, we'll base it on the model and the concept art."

Previz, or low-resolution previsualization animation, is a planning tool for the animation, but can also be used as a guideline for building miniatures and sets.

"Sometimes Peter is really enthusiastic about a maquette or a piece of artwork. However, from the animation point of view, it's often necessary to have a certain pathway—which we call a red carpet—very accurately matched to the previz. It saves a lot of time for the animators if the contours of the landscape exactly match when they swap out their computer environment and swap in the miniature environment." In other words, if the miniature and previz environments match in red-carpet areas, Kong's feet should touch the ground with little adjustment to the animation.

"Our miniature-building is very organic—we're

Working on a wall miniature.

Working on the cathedral miniature.

assembled from separate stones that you could pluck out one at a time. "You can't because it's part of a big sheet," says John. "It's all molded, plus a little bit of hand-carving. We got a whole lot of nice-looking stones and smashed them up. Then we physically built a piece of dry-stone wall, and we silicone-molded it. And then Duncan sprays insulation foam into the mold. We spliced this wall together out of foam panels."

The workshop has built up quite a library of silicone-molded imprints of real rocks from all over Wellington. Urethane sprayer Duncan Brown has been using the molds to produce huge amounts of rock texture over many months. "You can spray probably two tons of foam in a day if you were really going crazy," he guesses. "The most I've ever done was spray half a ton in three hours, which is a considerable amount of foam. It gives off a lot of gas." He laughs.

One mold can be used many times, but Duncan has tricks for giving each new panel a touch of individuality. The spraying machine, a Gusmer, has a fifty-foot hose with a gun on the end that comes with different-shaped tips. "You might get a big fan that sprays heaps or turn it down and just spray a small

stream so that it gets into all the crannies," he says, "and changing the temperature that you're spraying at changes the density of it, so you get different results."

"What Duncan does is very artistic," says John. "Although he's using a big industrial machine, he adapts what he's doing to get a certain look."

For the red-carpet sections of each miniature, the workshop has a precision router, a computer-guided cutting machine. "It looks pretty basic, but it can read a three-dimensional computer file," says John. He picks up a tiny airplane propeller and shows its smooth curves, all cut by the router. "The cutter goes up and down, sideways and lengthways, and can describe any shape in space. It's like a dentist drill on wheels. It cuts wood, polystyrene foam, aluminum . . ."

Today the router is being prepped to make a replica of a branch Naomi Watts sits on, on one of the live-action sets. The live-action version was carefully mapped by the set surveyors, who use a theodolite, a surveying instrument, to precisely measure the contours of each set. Coordinates describing the shape of the branch will be loaded into the router's computer. "That branch is going to be made by the router in 3D, exactly how it was on set," says John. "We can be more artistic and free where we're outside of the red-carpet realm, but where we have to be accurate, we can be one hundred percent accurate. It's a perfect world."

Of course, Ann's branch is not the only bit of tree on Skull Island. Weta Workshop's greens department has been building a jungle-load of miniature trees, vines, mosses, and ferns—twenty-thousand ferns to be precise.

"So how do you make miniature ferns?" ponders greens supervisor Dave Goodin. "You starve them and confine what they have to grow in."

The greens team collected small ferns, about fifty millimeters (two inches) high—baby ferns or ferns stunted by tough environments. "We brought them back to a nursery in the Hutt Valley . . . and we'd put up to eight ferns into a fifty-millimeter-by-fifty-millimeter pot with a [ladies'] stocking inside it. . . . Then we'd put a tablespoon of no-nutrient soil in with them. We bought boxes and boxes, thousands of stockings . . . little sacks that the ferns have lived in now for over twelve months. They'd have something to live on so they wouldn't die, but they didn't grow. And so eventually we had these wonderful little ferns. The smallest are probably about seventy millimeters from tip to tip."

Three greens teamsters have been heading for

Detail of maquette foliage and rock.

the hills regularly to harvest dwarfed trees and tree components from the Orongorongos, a mountain range about three hours' drive from Wellington. "We go to a private property, a big sheep station on the South Wairarapa coast," says Dave. "It's freezing cold and it's usually covered in mist, so you're blind, crawling around looking for little ferns or climbing trees to get branches—no more than two branches off any one tree." In the last year and a half, quite a few branches have passed through Weta Workshop's gates.

Each miniature tree is assembled from bits of real trees, polystyrene foam, spring wire, plasticine, and plastic leaves. A mini tree's fine branches might be grafted from one tree, and its gnarly trunk from another, since a single real branch is unlikely to look right for both. "You need to make things taper quickly from the roots to the tip of the branches," Dave explains. "We've only got a meter to make all that reduction."

The trees have been made to a variety of scales, some being almost ten feet tall. "We've made tenth-scale trees, twentieth-scale trees, right down to ninetieth scale," says Dave. "Our biggest trees were thirty meters in real life, and at tenth scale were three meters. Our smallest trees, although they look thirty meters in real life on the screen, were only about three hundred millimeters high. The different scales of trees are used on the same set. It's about forcing perspective."

Forced perspective creates a sense of distance, so that the far end of a miniature chasm or gorge can look miles away. "Closer to the camera we have the bigger trees, and we put the smaller trees in the back, so that when you look at it on the screen and the mist and the fog have been added, it creates that feeling of a vast landscape, a huge distance. You force the perspective. It is not what is right, it's what looks right."

Peter Jackson wants Skull Island to have a hot,

steamy, windy look. He wants the foliage to feel alive—waving in the breezes, buffeted by the strong winds. But animating miniature trees in a wind-blown way is not a simple matter of just aiming a fan at them. "A small tree has got short limbs," Dave points out. "If you get a small tree that's a meter high and try to make the branches move, it just wobbles."

Getting the trees to move in an appropriate way was initially something of a nightmare for the greens team. But New Zealanders pride themselves on still having something of a pioneer spirit: they reckon they can make just about anything out of fencing wire. So the solution was to cut the branches off each tree and reconnect them with a short length of spring-steel wire, then pad out and paint over the wire section to match the rest of the branch. Over on the miniatures shooting stage, model technicians can further control the quality of the motion by adding tiny weights to the tips of some branches so that, when the fans are turned on, there's the right sort of rustling, variegated drag and flow to the movement of the foliage.

Dave has no idea how many leaves have been attached to the miniature trees: "Trillions! We haven't counted." He laughs. "Weta Workshop sent two people to China, and they brought back two shipping containers full of plastic plant components that we thought would help make the jungle. Real leaves are far out of scale, and so we use plastic leaves. We put on a canopy of leaves that are in scale with the tree."

The countless vines and roots tangling and snaking across the Skull Island landscape look like fun to make. Dave picks up a hose of soft, white

Top: Rob Gillies working on miniature trees. Below: Dan Aird working on a miniature that combines a tree with ruined architecture.

123

polyurethane foam hanging from a hook in the greens workshop. "In this jungle, a lot of trees have aerial roots that come down. This foam is used in the real world—when you put aluminum windows into a house, you squeeze it between the house and the window to stop the draft." He lines it up beside a painted, shriveled, textured root that was once a length of the same smooth, white foam. "It's heat-gunned to shrink it and create its texture. The foam has got airholes in it. With the heat gun you're exploding those little bubbles and it collapses on itself." He rolls the root against the bench with his hand to show how the end can easily be tapered. With a bit of wire inside to shape it, it will be ready to be glued to a tree trunk.

A lot of artificial vines are brought in from China, but Dave likes the ones his team makes better. "This is latex rubber," he says, picking up a thin, flexible vine. "We spray liquid latex out into a sheet and it dries in about twenty minutes, then we pick up the edge of the latex and roll it." It has a weight and consistency that allow it to drape nicely from tree to tree. Some of the latex vines have wire inside. "When we roll them up, we roll florist's wire into the latex, so then you can pose it and it stays, and it has kinks in it."

The Skull Island jungle is centuries old, and the greens team has been making trees that look their age. "You can't just make a whole lot of neat-looking trees, all pristine," says Dave. "You've got to make a living jungle, which actually means parts of it are dying or dead."

One dead-looking tree is standing on a workbench. "This is made from a stump that I found on the beach. Yesterday, I didn't like this tree, it didn't look right, it looked too new down at the bottom. So I carved this big hole and made it hollow. And I put steel wool in there, so it's like 'Ooh, don't go in there—spiderwebs,' to make it look creepy, because this is a creepy movie."

Weta Workshop, with its caves and flora and other delights, is an enchanting miniature wonderland. As you step outside its gates, you find yourself looking at the real world with fresh eyes—seeing the textures of bark and rock, the numbers of leaves on trees, and the way branches move in the wind.

Dan Aird shaping a miniature (1:30 scale) tree.

Keri Manuel and Paul Van Ommen working on an articulated miniature tree.

Miniature of the Ruined Valley.

"Part of the charm of miniatures," says Alex Funke, "is that you control the whole world."

Alex is director of photography for visual effects, heading a team that is filming vast chunks of Skull Island in miniature: the deep ravine of the log chasm, the full height of the great wall, the fight clearing where Kong battles the V-Rexes, the vine chasm, the slippery slope, Kong's lair, and much, much more.

"There simply isn't enough time or money to build a live-action set that actually goes as far as the eye can see," he says. "You can build a miniature that is six or ten meters deep and it literally *will* be as far as the eye can see, once they put a little bit of haze in there."

But even if the art department could build the entire wall, one-to-one scale, there is something appealing about making it in miniature. "Peter's always said if he wasn't a director, he'd be a miniature cameraman," says Alex. "All his life he's been a completely hands-on film-maker. He's built the miniatures, he's shot the miniatures . . . he loves this stuff! He's like a kid with a big toy-train set."

The miniatures shooting studio, tucked in on one end of Wellington Airport's runway, is a nondescript shed housing four stages, all of them in use.

Stage K is currently home to a section of the Brontosaur gorge, where a herd of stampeding Brontosaurs will run down Carl Denham and crew in one of the most thrilling, helter-skelter scenes of the movie.

The gorge looks like an enormously long trough. Its roughly shaped boxy exterior is made of plain, white slabs of polystyrene. The interior surfaces, beautifully painted and intricately detailed to look like rock, are dressed with myriad small trees and twined roots, tiny ferns, and touches of moss. The trough is just wide enough to walk through—waist-deep at one end, head-high at the other. Right now, the perfect illusion of a vast chasm is shattered by the presence of a model technician, squatting halfway along, arranging the greenery.

"The key to a successful miniatures unit is that everybody has to be fascinated with storytelling," says Alex. "It's not just a case of 'I've got this many square feet of moss to apply before I go home.' The guys who are the shepherds of this set, who work on it day after day, are so involved in the fine detailing—the fact that one rock is always in the sun so nothing grows on it, but underneath it, where it's a little damper, there's a little bit of moss. How does this work in terms of the context? Where is this environment? Is it dry, is it

# IT'S A SMALL, WINDY WORLD

Mary Maclachlan, Weta Workshop miniatures technician, working on an environmental design maquette.

wet, is it windy? Is it shadowed? Is there a side of the wall of this canyon that never gets the sun, so there are a lot more damp-loving plants growing there? I've been very fortunate to have a group of people who want to build those fine details into the storytelling."

Like all of the Skull Island environments, the gorge will certainly have to be windy. Getting the trees and ferns on the miniature sets to move in the wind in a natural way is extremely difficult, involving a complex equation of flexibility, weight, and speed. The first part of the problem has been solved by inserting flexible rods into the stiff little branches of the miniature trees. "Which is great," says Alex, "except now the branches don't have the right mass. They're too light. They bend properly, but they just tend to jitter in the wind."

Some well-placed fishing sinkers solved the problem of the too fluttery foliage. Scott Harens, special effects supervisor at the miniatures unit, came up with the idea of clamping tiny lead shots onto leaves and fern fronds to weigh them down. That extra mass serves to slow their movement as air breezes through them.

Weighting some of the foliage gave the plants just the right combination of bending, swaying, and fluttering movements, but they still moved too

quickly to give a truly convincing illusion of full-size trees in motion. The final touch was to speed up the film in the camera. "Instead of shooting at twenty-four frames per second, we shoot at sixty-four frames. How did we get that number? Pure empirical experiment: we did a lot of videos at different speeds, and we finally settled at sixty-four frames a second." Played back at normal speed, the movement of branches and weighted leaves slows right down to finally give the miniatures the stature of real trees.

"So we have a nest of problems—the problem of making the tree movement right, the problem of getting a camera speed that will make that miniature motion work, and then the problem of getting the motion-control rigs to go fast enough to make the camera moves. We pretty much tamed that," says Alex happily.

The miniatures crew has been shooting sections of the chasm for the Brontosaur chase for a couple of months and yet is still only halfway through the sequence. Today the crew will be shooting three shots in Stage K, including a 180-degree pan as Jack turns to look back at some carnosaurs chasing the brontosaurs. In the adjoining stage sits another stretch of the chasm, and the crew there is scheduled to shoot half a dozen shots today, including a low-angle shot to go with a digital carnosaur leaping over the camera, and a shot of the chasm floor as Hayes runs over it.

The shots are extremely complex technically. Each one needs to match a previz version, and frequently also a live-action version. Many, many of the shots of Skull Island consist of a live-action foreground, a miniature middle ground, and a digital background, and each of these elements must merge seamlessly within the shot. And that means matching miniature and live-action sets, complementing lighting, and replicating camera moves.

A small section of the chasm was built as a live-

Brontosaur stampede miniature environment plate.

Digital reference terrain wireframe over miniature plate.

action set out at Windy Point. "For one part of the Brontosaur chase, they built just the ground that the actors run on—a detailed piece of pavement about thirty to forty meters long, but it's just the floor. There's no chasm. And along the edge of that floor is a blue wall. So our wall has to very accurately follow the edge of that built ground plan," explains Alex.

Where the sets need to meet, the miniature set has been built to match the live-action set exactly, using survey information provided by the on-set survey department. Set surveyors use a theodolite—a tool traditionally used in the construction and roading industries for measuring angles and distance—to map the positions of particular points on the set. Computer software translates that data into a series of points in virtual space, then joins up the dots to create a 3D line drawing, a digital representation of the contours of the set.

The surveyors also measure the positions of the live-action cameras in relation to the set, so the digital camera department can precisely track the camera moves. That information is sent to the animators, who set up virtual cameras and animate the Brontosaurs to run on virtual surfaces that match the miniature or live-action sets that will eventually replace them.

Updated previz is then sent to the miniatures unit, along with computer files for the motion-control rigs guiding the unit's cameras. "This is what we call plug and play, which we also call plug and pray!" says Alex, laughing. "The idea is that they take the behavior of a virtual camera, and they export it as numbers to our motion control. We should be able to drop it into the motion control, turn it on, and it'll do exactly what the digital camera did. We tell the camera to go where the first frame is, and if we're lucky, it goes there and doesn't end up inside the wall!"

Sometimes, just fitting a full-scale camera into a tenth-scale set can be tricky. To replicate the movement of a camera traveling at knee height on the live-action set, part of the miniatures camera might need to be traveling impossibly through the ground. Currently, the camera in Stage K is mounted on a boom reaching over the bronto chasm, with a snorkel lens dangling into the gorge like an upside-down periscope.

Giving the camera access into the set sometimes means reconfiguring the camera rig for a shot, or adjusting the parameters of the movement in the motion-control file. Often it means carving up the miniature.

"There's a lot of challenge, a lot of decision-making, when the set's in on the stage," says Paul Van Ommen, head of department for models and modelmaking within the miniatures unit. "We're dealing with tenth scale, and you have a camera package that has to fit within that set, and you have a rig to move it, and often we chop large sections of the set away in order for us to get the rig in. We've even had camera moves where we're moving a piece of set away with another motion control rig, just so that we can get in there. Then, as the camera comes out, that other bit of set gets moved back in."

And then there is the lighting: Peter Jackson might want one scene to be dark and murky, another to be shadowy with shafts of sunlight. Alex Funke's lighting schemes for the miniatures often need to complement those of his on-set counterpart, director of photography Andrew Lesnie. Andrew's lighting setups are documented by lighting continuity man Ants Farrell. "Instead of having to call someone and say, 'You know that shot you did three months ago? What color blue did you have on the backlight? . . . Oh, you're not sure?' I can pull up Ants's documentation and see that the key light had such and such a gel on and it was flooded this much and how bright it was," says Alex.

Currently in Stage L is the fight clearing, a relatively flat piece of land where Kong fights the V-Rexes. It is one of many miniature sets for the thrilling battle, during which Kong, V-Rexes, and Ann tumble down the vine chasm into a swamp. Alex estimates that the completed sequence will run for about ten minutes, and the action (mostly digital) takes place entirely on miniature sets, except for

some live-action footage of Naomi Watts filmed in green-screen limbo.

"The fight between Kong and the V-Rexes was the first sequence that we started on," says Alex. "Many of the shots are actually exact copies of the original film, so you have to look at the original and see how much Peter has carried over—in terms of design style, in terms of composition. We're very conscious that Willis O'Brien and the guys who did the original film really knew what they were doing."

Willis O'Brien, the special effects pioneer behind the original *King Kong*, shot the battle as a "proof of concept," a demonstration sequence to prove that a movie could be done with stop-motion puppets. "On the original *Kong*, it was the very first thing that went onto camera, and in homage to that, we started with that too."

Along one side of the miniatures studio runs an annex. It is crowded with rows of miniature trees, racks of vines and roots, trays of tiny ferns and mosses, and piles of rocks—all ready for a turn on set.

The miniature trees have also been filmed individually. "Each one has been shot by itself against a blue screen, as a separate freestanding piece," says Alex. "It's been shot in multiple angles of rotation, multiple lighting schemes, looking up at the tree, looking down at the tree, so you have a vast library of trees that are in motion, because these are all trees that we put wind on. So now you can build a digital background, but put into that these actual shots of these moving trees. So it's a matte painting with motion in it.

"This is no fantasy. As far as Peter is concerned, Skull Island is a real place. By using live action, a miniature set, a matte painting with miniature and live-action elements, and a true matte painting, four layers deep, you can build shots as complex and detailed as the real world."

Working on the first Skull Island wall miniature.

Peter Jackson advises Naomi Watts on a section of a Skull Island interior set.

Even without its New York City and ocean sequences, *King Kong* would be a huge project for the digital effects teams at Weta Digital, as the film's middle act is set entirely on Skull Island. "Peter Jackson's concept of Skull Island is this incredibly overgrown, lush jungle that doesn't exist anywhere," says Ben Snow, visual effects supervisor. "It really is the jungle from hell."

Every live-action and miniature set for Skull Island has had huge blue or green screens in the background. Those screens must eventually be replaced with digital landscapes extending Skull Island into the distance.

But it's not just a matter of filling in the horizon with a digital painting. As the digital effects teams meld the live-action and miniature sets into single environments, they are adding extra details and atmosphere into the middle ground and foreground.

Take the great wall, for instance, where Ann is delivered into Kong's domain. A large section of the wall is a miniature, while other small parts are live-action sets, with actors torching short rivers of fire. The digital effects team will stitch the miniature and live-action pieces of the wall together, stoke up the fires and smoke, put digital Skull Islanders on the miniature parts of the wall, extend the rivers of flame to flow down the wall, and set an immense skull ablaze.

"We'll completely dress it to make it look gigantic," says digital effects supervisor Eric Saindon. "We'll add atmosphere and all the other elements that are going to bring it to life and really sell it as a giant element on this island."

Right now, Eric's team is concentrating on the Kong versus V-Rex battle sequence, which he anticipates will run to four hundred shots. The miniatures unit has spent months filming miniature environments for the sequence, including a deep chasm into which Ann and the monsters tumble down through masses of vines. The creatures, of course, are digital, and most of the vines will be digital too, but the art department also made some actual vines just for Ann. "We have lots of footage of her just swinging back and forth in the vines. And at the very bottom there's the Ann swamp set, which was probably thirty feet by thirty feet. . . . So that set will pop right down in the middle of our miniatures set and we'll have to combine the two into one."

Skull Island is a patchwork of live-action, miniature, and digital elements. If all goes according to plan, the audience will not be able to tell what is real and what is not, whether a waterfall in the distance has been computer-generated or

## THE PATCHWORK ISLAND

144

Top: Miniature at 1:10 scale.
Below: Miniature set.

A shot from the final film shows all the patchwork elements brought together.

shot in the wild. As Kong and the V-Rexes crash through the miniature jungle, as the Brontosaurs rampage through the chasm, some of the grasses and trees and rocks that bend or break or tumble will be digital; some will be live-action rocks and grasses, shot as separate elements against blue screen, with a blue-screened weight (representing a giant foot or arm) slamming into them, bending them, shattering them.

"It's a kind of marrying of all these mixed elements that were all taken from different places," says 2D sequence supervisor Erik Winquist. "Some of these composites can get pretty complicated, with fifty layers or so of different little bits and pieces that are all locked to this moving camera."

Of course, with every miniature and live-action set shot against blue or green screen, none of the skies in *King Kong* are real. "We are creating the entire sky," says Ben Snow. "But you want to have whatever you create rooted in some sort of reality. We send people out to take a lot of photographs of different skies, and from that we'll stitch together [our] sky. It's a bunch of photographs made into a big circular dome, and then a matte painter might go in and add some details to make it better than perfect. Then we'll sometimes animate it, put a little bit of motion

in to get some movement in the clouds." It's like putting a cap on top of the world.

Long before the digital effects teams began stitching together all the fragments of rock, sky, and jungle, Peter Jackson could see the whole picture. "Peter has it in his head what it's going to look like," says Erik. "Big credit to the actors and to Peter to shoot something that has so little reality in it, and then suddenly it ends up looking amazing. Suddenly you can start totally believing that this is an amazingly huge, whole world."

Erik is working to ensure that the completed shots of Skull Island capture the spirit of the concept artwork. "We'll fill everything out to give it depth, to make it look a lot like the original *King Kong*. So there'll be vines that are very dark draping through the foreground. Where the action is happening, it'll be light, and in the very background it'll be very bright, blown out—just like the layering of the glass paintings from the original movie."

Translating the stylized artwork to photo-realistic film has its challenges. "If you make it look too much like the artwork, then it looks like something very synthetic. But if you make it too realistic, then you lose a lot of the spirit of the artwork. We have to try and find a balance between this romantic vision of Skull Island and making it believable as a real place."

Left: Weta sign made from No. 8 wire and barbed wire, built by Dave Irons and Alex Falkner. Right: Weta Workshop reception area.

The weta, say the people at Weta Workshop, is "New Zealand's coolest little monster, a bizarre and prickly prehistoric cricket." There's a big one, fashioned out of fencing wire, crawling out of a hole in the Weta Workshop sign outside the main entrance.

Weta Workshop is Creature Central. Lurtz, an Uruk-hai from *The Lord of the Rings*, stands guard at the door, menacing visitors with a malevolent glare. Pitiful Gollum, with baleful eyes, sits clutching his fish. Dragons and orcs lurk in corridors, fantasy figurines line shelves and cabinets, skulls and skeletons add to the clutter of work tools, sketch pads, and reference books on tables and benches.

On the coffee table at reception, Kong is locked in battle with three V-Rexes. His back is arched, his teeth are bared. With one hand, he is wrenching apart the jaws of a V-Rex. He is stomping the second into the mud and roots underfoot. He carries Ann aloft in his other hand, just out of reach of the third V-Rex's snapping jaws.

Nine years ago, Richard Taylor, head of Weta Workshop, sculpted this scene to show the dynamics of the battle between Kong and the three dinosaurs. "It was purely a conceptual piece," he says, "which we sent off to Universal to try and inspire them to what this film could be."

Back in 1997, Universal shelved the project, but not before Weta Workshop had gone a substantial way toward designing the creatures of Skull Island. The plan was to bring the creatures to life using a combination of animatronics, stop-motion puppetry, and digital effects. "We were sculpting our first animatronic puppet, because, back then, our digital arm was not yet at the strength it is today," says Richard. "We had built a large number of stop-animation puppets of Kong, the brontosaurs, the V-Rexes, the sailors."

Since then, with the extensive use of digital effects in *The Lord of the Rings* trilogy, Weta's digital arm has gone from strength to strength, so this time around, the creatures are almost all digital. The one exception is a large, flightless bird, seen as it gasps its last breath, having just been shot by the *Venture* crew. It was built as a physical puppet with radio-controlled eyes. A couple of puppeteers lay underneath it on set, one wearing its legs, the other with his hand inside its head.

Weta Workshop and Weta Digital are sister companies, and the job of creating the creatures is a joint effort, with the Workshop often spearheading the initial design process.

"On *King Kong* we have done more drawings than I think we've ever done before," says Richard, "and it's arguable that we may have done more conceptual art

# WETA WORLD

than almost any feature film before. . . . We have done thousands of illustrations. And then we have done hundreds of design maquettes. For two years, they were just pouring out of the design department."

A maquette is a study model. Once Peter Jackson is happy with the way a creature design is shaping up on paper, the design team explores the design further by sculpting small plasticine design maquettes.

"Peter doesn't need to lock down on a drawing," says Richard. "He just needs to suggest that the drawing has the right aesthetic. At that point we'll make a junction into 3D sculpting and begin conceptualizing in the round. As a director, Peter really enjoys the opportunity to see art in the round, so he can understand three-dimensionally what these creatures look like. Then once he approves the design maquette, the next process for us is to turn it into a scannable maquette, and this is a massive part of our job on *Kong*. We have had a very large resource of people creating these creatures as scannable maquettes for two years."

The scannable maquette is a larger-scale sculpture, usually several feet tall and much more detailed than the design maquette. It is sculpted in plasticine, then molded and cast in urethane, resulting in a hard copy that can then be scanned three-dimensionally onto a computer and sent as a digital file to Weta Digital for transformation into a full-fledged movable digital creature.

"The creatures in Skull Island have to be believable, but can be wildly rich in their design, and that's a nice aesthetic to find," says Richard. "We didn't feel a necessity to be accurate to the latest knowledge from dinosaur experts around the world. We felt we had license to make our creatures more fantastical, almost Ray Harryhausenesque, because Skull Island has been frozen in time for sixty-five million years, so

evolution has continued on. Our dinosaurs can actually be sixty-five million years different to when *Jurassic Park* discovered their dinosaurs. So that gave us a license. Peter's enthusiasm for film has been borne on the back of Willis O'Brien's work, Marcel Delgado's work, and Ray Harryhausen's work. So it's been lovely to bring this fantastical aspect to the realties of our creatures."

Designing the look of Kong himself required careful consideration of his circumstances and character. "We visualized Kong almost as if he was a broken Quasimodo-like figure," says Richard. "He's atrophied in his face, he's slobbering, smelly, almost destitute. He has almost grown insane with loneliness. He hasn't communicated with another primate for sixty years. And then Ann is there, and Ann allows Kong to grow in strength of character from this broken creature into the alpha male of the island again. Ann gives him a necessity to fight, and that brings out of him a need to rise again to be the mightiest of the island, to vanquish all of his foes, because he has to protect this creature that is now, in some way, relating with him. Of course, that is then dramatically reversed as Kong is brought down and destroyed, only to rise one last time to climb the Empire State Building as the alpha male. It's a very interesting story path that we have to communicate visually in the face of Kong, in his persona, his body, and in how he'll perform. It's a very complex design issue: do it short of the mark and we'll have a hollow and shallow creature that has no empathetic relationship with the audience; overdo it and you'll have an overly theatrical creature that is potentially laughable. Fit it in the middle, in the right spot, and hopefully we'll create a memorable, beautiful, filmic creature, on a par with something like Gollum."

148

River raft creature concepts

(1)

(2)

(3)

Gus Hunter's concepts for the Piranhadon swamp creature.

Left to right: Gary Hunt, Sam Belcher, Don Brooker, Steve Unwin, and Christian Pearce working on the Pirhanadon swamp creature maquette for scanning.

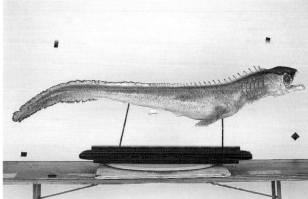

Painted scannable maquette of Pirhanadon swamp creature.

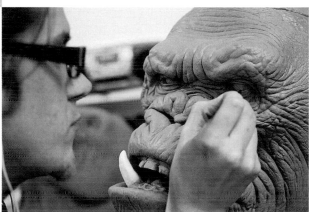

Jamie Beswarick sculpting the Kong aggressive face study.

Clockwise: Greg Broadmore creature concept for V-Rex. Christian Pearce creature concept for V-Rex.
Greg Broadmore concept for V-Rex.

Only one creature design from the 1996 preproduction phase has made it into the 2005 version of *King Kong*: the brontosaur.

"Pretty much everything else was designed from scratch," says Weta Workshop concept designer Greg Broadmore. "We did hundreds and hundreds of drawings and sculpts. And there were dozens more for all the creatures that didn't make it into the film as well."

The team took a scattergun approach, putting every idea down on paper, no matter how weird or wacky. They worked independently, dashing off rough pencil sketches, then scanning the drawings into their computers and coloring them in Photoshop.

"We were concentrating on not doing what the other guy was doing at first," says conceptual designer Christian Pearce, "rather than trying to get cohesive before we put anything in front of Peter."

"I probably did twenty or thirty different V-Rex designs," says Greg. "To start with, I wanted to just draw the coolest V-Rex I could think of."

"Greg and I were big dinosaur fans before *King Kong*, big fans of *Jurassic Park*," says Christian. "But we didn't want our rex looking like the *Jurassic Park* rex."

Peter Jackson's responses to their first illustrations gave the designers a clear sense of directions to explore. He liked one drawing of a V-Rex with rotten meat hanging out of its teeth and another with its eye poked out.

"We quickly realized that Peter wanted the most evil, diabolical, monstrous V-Rex you could imagine," says Greg. "It wasn't about making it a real dinosaur. It was about making it the most terrifying thing that Kong could fight. We worked on making the eyes scary, and making it nasty and smelly—which is a recurring theme in this movie!" He laughs.

"There was talk early on of the rex being a lot more upright, like in Charles Knight's old paintings, where it used to walk around like a man with his tail dragging along the ground," says Christian.

"Charles Knight was a famous dinosaur artist, one of the original dinosaur artists who still influences today," says Greg. "A lot of his old dinosaurs were crocodilian, reptilian, and had traits that aren't represented in dinosaurs anymore. The modern scientific dinosaur has very fine scales, but Pete wanted it to be more archaic, so I asked if he wanted the crocodile scales. To put crocodile scales on a dinosaur is kind of ludicrous, but it makes it look cooler and gives it an older-fashioned Ray Harryhausenesque look."

The decision to go with a crocodilian

## THE CREATURES

Greg Broadmore creature concept for V-Rex.

another one turns up and it's gnarlier and scarier than the last one. And finally the third one turns up and it's the biggest of all. We wanted them not just to be bigger and nastier, but to have their own individual qualities.

"We thought of them as this group of ornery yokels, this inbred family of dinosaurs—the matriarch, the bull, and the juvenile. We really wanted the matriarch to be this beaten-up, old, grizzled character. Everything about her is a bit more withered and sunken in than the others. She's starting to sag. Her torso and tail are hanging lower than her hips. The bull is heavily muscled and has this big butting kind of heavy-boned head. And the juvenile is slimmer,

skin texture cost the production hundreds of man-hours. "They were such a time-consuming thing to sculpt," reveals Christian. "But it was a great defining characteristic which really separates it from the *Jurassic Park* rex—that heavy scaling running down its back."

The designers played around with scarring to give the V-Rexes a battle-hardened look. One V-Rex was drawn with a raking of scars across its muzzle, which Greg figures could have been picked up in a fight or perhaps during eating. "I'd imagine that it had just pulled its head out of a rib cage," he says. "The way it feeds, it would just jam its head into another dead creature and get out what it could, but as it's going through all the bones, it's damaging itself. V-Rexes don't care about those little injuries. It's just a skin wound for a V-Rex.

"We were always trying to rationalize everything," Greg says, laughing, "definitely trying to ground it in reality, because as crazy as you go with your design, at the end of the day you've got to pull it back to something that works.

"Peter wanted the V-Rexes to be three different characters," Greg says. "You see one V-Rex try to attack Ann, and you think, 'oh my God, it's almost bigger than Kong.' And then suddenly, what the hell,

Greg Broadmore size comparison of V-Rex bull, matriarch, and male juvenile.

more graceful, more poised, and he has a more classic dinosaur posture where he's very horizontal. There was tons of work in making them individuals."

"None of these are real rexes as we know them, but they have the basic traits of large theropods," says Christian. "My guys were a little more front-heavy than Greg's were. He always seemed to put the weighting of the rex further behind the hips than I did. I always tried to have that forward-heavy aspect to it to give him that lower-down head, which to me looks more aggressive and spookier.

"It was a pretty intense illustrative period, but once it had gotten past the first two passes with Peter, it got taken over by the sculptors, and they did so much of the work themselves. None of the V-Rex drawings show that thin, nimble waist that they ended up with, for instance. So much was resolved in the sculpt."

Ann Darrow and Jack Driscoll escape from Kong's lair with the unlikely aid of a Terapusmordax flying creature. "That was a fun one," says Christian. "You could just try anything you wanted. Warren, another of the conceptual designers, was working from out of town and we'd get a shipment from him every couple of days: 'Oh, my goodness! Look what he was thinking! Let's steal some of those ideas.' And he'd get ours and some of those ideas would trigger things in him too. It was right towards the end of the creature design process. We were all fighting to get our little bits into this guy. I think a bit of all of us ended up in it.

"Infected-looking was what Peter kept mentioning. Right from the start we were talking about naked mole rats, which are hideous-looking little creatures. That was a basis for

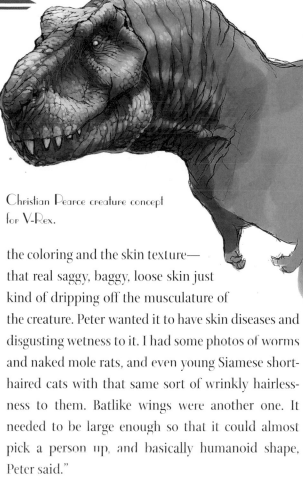

Christian Pearce creature concept for V-Rex.

the coloring and the skin texture— that real saggy, baggy, loose skin just kind of dripping off the musculature of the creature. Peter wanted it to have skin diseases and disgusting wetness to it. I had some photos of worms and naked mole rats, and even young Siamese short-haired cats with that same sort of wrinkly hairless-ness to them. Batlike wings were another one. It needed to be large enough so that it could almost pick a person up, and basically humanoid shape, Peter said."

Not all of the designs were entirely practical. "There were some where the wings were mounted on its back legs," says Christian, "which caused a bit of an uproar amongst some of the zoologists here, who said that creatures can't fly with their back legs. But we were just putting everything out there, trying new things to see what's going to catch Peter's eye."

"In one of the more preposterous ones I did," says Greg, "I gave it a big, gross belly, which I thought was kind of funny, but it did make it less likely as a flying creature. So it

Terapusmordax flying creature concept by Greg Broadmore.

ended up thin. In the end, on the final scannable maquette, we pushed it even further, made it as emaciated as possible."

Exploring the look of a creature raises questions about its lifestyle, its diet, or where it lives on the island, and the answers all affect the design. "Whenever we talk to Peter, he'll give us little tidbits of what the creature gets up to and what it needs to be able to do," says Christian. "The Terapusmordax flying creature was going to be living up in the mountains, and it seems to be a guy who's quite social—they go out hunting in packs. They've got big, strong feet and sicklelike toes, which they use for hunting and for hanging upside down from the roof like a bat."

"Peter really drove us a long way with the flying creature," says Greg. "He kept on pushing us. In the end he came back with this idea of it having skin like a sphinx cat . . . and we started introducing little sores and making them horrible, scabby little creatures, and that was a great deal of fun.

"You try to think of every trick that makes it disgusting, what grosses you out, and what grosses Peter out. In one drawing I tried to take it to an absolute extreme, as foul as I could make it, in this pile of yellow sludge like it's practically melting—grotesque, all inflamed, with varicose veins under the skin. Then we did rabbit variants, which are much more rodent-

like and doglike, and Pete really liked the taut skin over the rib cage with all the excess skin around the joints, and just how . . . diseased it looked."

Once Peter was happy with the look of the Terapusmordax flying creature's body, the designers sculpted a small design maquette in plasticine and then experimented with different heads for it. "We did probably twenty or thirty sculptures just of the head," says Greg. "We nailed down various characteristics from the different sculpts—the teeth from one and skull of another. And even when we started sculpting the head on the final scannable maquette, there were revisions."

The huge, predatory Piranhadon swamp creature that knocks the sailors off their rafts was based on an early illustration by conceptual artist Gus Hunter. Although Peter liked Gus's concept, he asked the designers to explore variations.

Terapusmordax flying creature scannable maquette.

Terapusmordax flying creature design maquette.

"I was looking at seal anatomy for its fins. It needed quite a strong torso and limbs to support itself on the water," says Christian. "The head was always inspired by those deep-sea angler fish with those long, pointy teeth. And the large eyes are also a low-light deep-sea feature, which probably doesn't make a lot of sense for a swamp-based creature, but he's a cool-looking guy. For all the going around the block that it did, it ended up staying pretty close to Gus's original drawing. Gus almost nailed it right from the get-go."

Many of the incidental creatures of Skull Island, such as insects, centipedes, and a Scorpiopede, were quickly designed and quickly approved. "A lot of these drawings, Peter [approved] on the first pass and gave them to the digital guys, who built them straight in the computer. There were no sculpts of them done here," says Christian.

When Kong knocks Ann's would-be rescuers off the log spanning a deep chasm, they fall into a pit full of all sorts of vile creatures. The scene in the pit was almost, but not quite, in the original film, says Greg. "In the 1933 *King Kong* when they fall into the pit, as they hit the ground, you kind of see a couple of shapes in spidery forms, and Jack Driscoll fights off a lizardy creature at the end, but you don't really get to see it because it was cut from the film, and unfortunately that footage was lost. But Pete wanted to reinstate it in his version of the film because he thought it was a great terrifying moment. So we got to design lots of creepy, crawly, insecty creatures. I'm really looking forward to the pit sequence. It's really scary. There are probably half a dozen different life-forms down there—mostly crustaceans, but also slugs and spidery things and a giant weta, which is very close to a real weta—it's kind of an überweta."

"We were trying to get crabs in the movie right from the get-go," says Christian. "Peter was only half-interested in them at the start, but a couple of our giant crabs ended up in the pit. We were both big crab fans before we started on this. They're just like little tanks that walk around, little armored dudes with these huge weapons out the front. They're pretty impregnable, and they can do a lot of damage. They seem like ready-made Skull Island locals."

Piranhadon swamp creature mouth detail.

Scorpiopede maquette designed and sculpted by Christian Pearce.

Steve Unwin and Bill Hunt blocking out the Terapusmordax flying creature.

The countless creature illustrations and experimental sculptures flying at top speed out of Weta Workshop's design room eventually whittled down to a Peter Jackson–approved design aesthetic for each creature. At that point, teams of sculptors began the painstakingly slow process of handcrafting intricately detailed scannable maquettes in plasticine.

"We've done ten or twelve scannable maquettes," says Richard Taylor. "Some of them will take five or six months for up to six people to sculpt—so the equivalent to building multiple miniatures in labor. But it's imperative that we capture all of the finest details, because a sculpture that we're doing six foot long will ultimately be thirty-six foot long on the screen, so it needs hyperdetail put into the finest textures, and the structural integrity and zoological aspects of the creatures must be sound.

"It's suggested that a lot is lost if you don't have an individual's inspiration in a piece," he continues. "We disagree here at Weta. We believe that there is a lovely enhancing of ideas by having a collaborative process. We'll have five or even six people— I liken them to hyenas around a carcass— sculpting on the one sculpture. And they rotate around the sculpt, so the sculpture stays as a live entity as it develops."

As the door to the sculpting room slides open, half a dozen faces look up from their workstations and smile cheerily. Here, every surface is cluttered with models, books, and hand tools. Creature and fantasy figurines, six to twelve inches high, sit in neat rows on out-of-reach shelves. Movie posters, concept art, and anatomical diagrams adorn walls and cupboards. A grisly, bloodied little human head, sculpted for a car seat commercial, sits in one corner.

# HYENAS AROUND THE CARCASS

The sculptors are busy crafting *King Kong* collectibles out of pinkish plasticine, each just a few inches high. One sculptor is working on a chess set, with Kong as king and Ann as queen. Two others are working on a pair of bookends. Another offers up his chair, sits down on a box, and continues scratching the back of a raptor.

"We're trying to get the merchandise finished up for the end of the month so we can get it all cast and molded and into stores by the time the movie comes out," says Bill Hunt, sculpting room supervisor, as he nicks at a V-Rex.

These tiny sculptures are among the smallest of the various models the team has done of the inhabitants of Skull Island. The scannable maquettes tend to be several feet tall, and the earlier and rougher design maquettes are typically ten to sixteen inches or so.

"Peter can go so far with drawings

and paintings, but then he needs something three-dimensional that he can move around and see how it's going to look to the camera and to the characters," says Bill. "Many of the design leaps are made during the maquette phase. There's lots of experimentation. Until you actually get something three-dimensional in front of you, there's only so much you can really explore, so a lot of design work continues on into—and beyond—sculpting. We've sculpted things, molded them, had them scanned, and then once Weta Digital gets the scan in the computer, Peter will still tweak it."

"Seven months until the film's released, and Kong has not been locked down yet," says sculptor Ben Hawker, as he etches a fur effect into the back of a mini-Kong. "His look, scale, head-to-body ratio—things are still in flux. . . . Everything has these rebirths. Peter will occasionally put his hands on something and start hacking. For the bull V-Rex, at one point he said, 'I need the head ten percent bigger.'"

"He just sliced off the front of the face and extended it and said, 'Yep, that's it,'" says Bill.

"We'd already got into the scales at that point," remembers Ben.

"The head was finished pretty much," says Bill. "Thankfully we were able to just fill in the gap. The front of the muzzle with all the detail was still there."

Seeing weeks—sometimes months—of painstaking work so suddenly and drastically rearranged can be frustrating. "It would be a lot more frustrating if Peter was ever wrong," says Bill, laughing, "but pretty much every time you see the change, you go, 'Well, he was right again!'"

"It can also be extremely elating when you've only got a few days to revamp this whole design, and you throw something together," says Ben. "Sometimes over a few days of passionate work you come up with pretty cool stuff."

All of the maquettes, no matter how big or small, start with some form of internal armature, a kind of stick figure made of twisted wire or rods of aluminum, steel, or brass, depending on the maquette's intended size. "The armatures for the scannable maquettes are very grunty," says Bill. "They're all welded together. For the smaller ones, you join the pieces together with a little bit of plumber's epoxy and you can make whatever pose you want. Richard Taylor says your sculpture's only as good as your armature.

"We use an oil-based plasticine, so it never dries out. It's a secret Weta blend. We keep using the same plasticine over and over again." Bill points to works in progress: "There are orcs in that Kong. There are *Frighteners* bodies in that one. It keeps getting melted down and reused. There's quite a legacy to the material." He laughs.

The sculptors have plenty of reference materials to inform their work: anatomy books, zoological texts.

"It's fantasy," says sculptor Ryk Fortuna, "but it's got strong roots based in naturalism and research."

"These creatures have evolved in the Skull Island universe," adds Ben. "They have to fit their environment. We give these creatures a backstory."

Where does this creature live? What does it eat?

Don Brooker at work on the V-Rex.

Johnny Brough helps the V-Rex matriarch take shape.

For the Terapusmordax flying creature that helps Ann and Jack escape from Kong's lair, the team first sculpted a muscle study—a maquette showing the creature without its skin—then sculpted the skin over the top. "That was to work out the anatomy," says Bill. "It's got a very translucent skin. You can almost see the organs and muscles inside it."

Sculpting complete creatures is not standard industry practice, says Bill: "A lot of people would just sculpt half of a creature. When you get it scanned, they can mirror the image in the computer so that you have a completely symmetrical creature. It cuts the sculpting time in half, which is a perk, but you end up with a creature that has a perfect straight line to its walk. We sculpted ours in the round, so there will be little imperfections. We did try as hard as we could to make their legs the same length, but you end up with a leg that's just a fraction longer than the other, so it's going to give it an irregular gait, which is more realistic."

"If it's too perfect," says Ryk, "it doesn't look right."

"Because nothing is symmetrical in nature," adds Bill. "Look at anybody's face."

The sculptors' individual sculpting styles make for slight differences too: "You've got one person working on one side of the tail, another working on

What does it need to survive to be a functioning creature? Bill explains that thinking through the answers to such questions gives them fresh ideas to put into the creatures. "The designs just come out of left field. We didn't have to religiously adhere to historical records. Our dinosaurs have been isolated, and they've had an extra sixty-five million years of evolution. Regular rexes don't have a waist, but we kept thinking of them as serpentine, running through these dense jungles and being able to wind between them, and they would need to be able to turn in the middle to be able to do that. So we've given them a waist."

The V-Rex's scales are also an adaptation to the dense Skull Island jungle environment. "They've got heavy plates on the legs to stop them from injuring themselves when they're running over trees and past rocks," says Ryk. "Even the aptitude of the claws—if they're running, they can get a great purchase in the ground, and the toes can spread out on a softer, marsh area."

"The bull is the Arnie, the Schwarzenegger of V-Rexes, so he's got a crest and is all bulked out," says Bill. "We're trying to make things that could actually exist—and look cool!"

Left to right: Steve Unwin, Greg Tozer, and Shaun Bolton at work on the Foetodon.

the other side, and you're working, working, working," says Ben. "Then when you look at the two sides—well, pick one and match up the other! But we keep rotating and putting on our own layers, almost like watercolor washes of texture. At the end of the day, all the pieces have a unified feeling and the stuff that comes out of here is better than anything any of us could have done alone."

"Shaun and Gary pretty well did one by themselves," says Bill. He calls out to Shaun Bolton in the far corner: "How long did the Lambeosaur scannable take?"

"About eight or nine months," says Shaun.

"About four months for the raptor," Bill calculates. "We did it quick." He laughs. "The matriarch, one of the V-Rexes, took six months."

"Most of the time was spent detailing them," says Ryk. "You can get the animal shape right quite quickly, but when it comes to laying out a detailed skin all over, you've got to look at how the creature is going to be moving. Every single scale on the rex has a dorsal fin and then little flutes and scratches. Where the scales brush against each other, they're flat and smooth, but on the back they're acting like a protective layer, so they tend to be chunkier with more relief to them."

"The matriarch was completely covered twice with scales, and then scratched off and redone," says Bill. "After six months of putting scales on a V-Rex—"

"—we've got scales printed on our retinas!" concludes Gary Hunt from his workstation behind a cupboard. "And then if you've been sculpting wrinkles, you'll be looking at someone, and you realize you're staring at their wrinkles!" A chorus of laughter suggests that he's not the only wrinkle-gazer.

Ben has laid out a range of small sculpting tools: an odd assortment of tiny hoops, blades, sponges, and brushes. Many are handmade, from wire, wood, and fretsaw blades. Some are modified dental tools. "You've got scratching tools for skin texture, blades for very fine detail like hairs, little ball-shaped things for pore texture." He fires up a butane torch and waves the flame over his sculpture. "The heat softens off all those cut marks. You can get forehead wrinkles with beautiful, soft little bevels. Then you put your pore texture in, and you scratch little lines between the pores."

"Gary used Glad wrap, or cling film as we call it in the U.K., on the raptor's skin," says Ryk. "You can sculpt through it, and it gives a softer, crisper, finer line."

Bill picks up a tool made from a crochet hook: "This was discovered by Greg Tozer round the corner there. It's really good for pore texture."

"Shaun pretty much uses just one tool," notes Ben.

"Shaun makes me feel like a sap," complains Bill. "I've got a huge box of tools and Shaun just uses one."

Shaun smiles serenely and continues nicking at the nose of a tiny Ann with his metal dental spatula.

"Here's one I've had since I was twelve!" Bill flourishes a little tool with a toothed metal loop and a battered handle. "I bought it in a kit of sculpting tools. It gets patched every three months."

Shaun Bolton and Greg Tozer at work on the Foetodon.

"Tools don't die," says Ben. "You just make them better."

Having the right tools is essential for such a time-intensive process. "Things don't just happen in a flash around here," says Ryk. "There's months of work. But that's what is so rewarding—to work so hard on something and watch it evolve and grow."

"Then when you finally see it on-screen," says Bill, "it's just unbelievable. We've seen a little test of the rexes walking around." In unison, the sculptors let out a whistle—clearly impressed and pleased at what Weta Digital has done with their creatures. "The first time that you see it in color, and the animators have not just made it move, but they've put character into it . . . They could have easily animated the three rexes all the same, but the character of their walks reflects what each one is, perfectly. You see that and think, 'Okay, that's what ten months of my life was about.'"

Just down the corridor from Weta Workshop's sculpting room, I come face-to-face with Kong. The workshop has built a loose sculptural study of Kong's face at full scale, six feet tall, so that Peter and the actors can get a sense of what it is like to look into the face of Kong. The effect is, in a word, awesome.

Weta Digital's Kong teams have referenced the enormous face too. "We've had a couple of groups coming over from Digital each week," says workshop supervisor Jason Docherty. "It's great for them to be able to see it in true scale and get a feel for it."

The face is really just a skin, made from sprayed urethane. It was scanned off the Kong scannable maquette, milled out of solid urethane, and then molded in silicone. "It took four or five weeks to go from having the sculpture to getting this reproduction," says Jason. "We did a thirty-thousand-dollar, eight-hundred-kilo mold—it was gigantic, the size of a large spa pool. Someone has been lowered into the mold on a harness and then sprayed it up in the same way they spray up all the rocks."

Despite its great size, the face only weighs about thirty or forty kilos, light enough to mount on a lighting stand with a wheeled base and a hand crank. It can be cranked twenty feet up to stand at Kong's true height and tilted to look down at Ann.

Also for reference, the workshop has produced smaller study models of Kong's hand and foot, as well as eighteen small expression studies of Kong's head, showing a range of facial expressions from passive to roaring.

Shaun Bolton and Sam Belcher detailing the Lambeosaur maquette.

Bill Hunt sculpting one of the eighteen facial expressions studies.

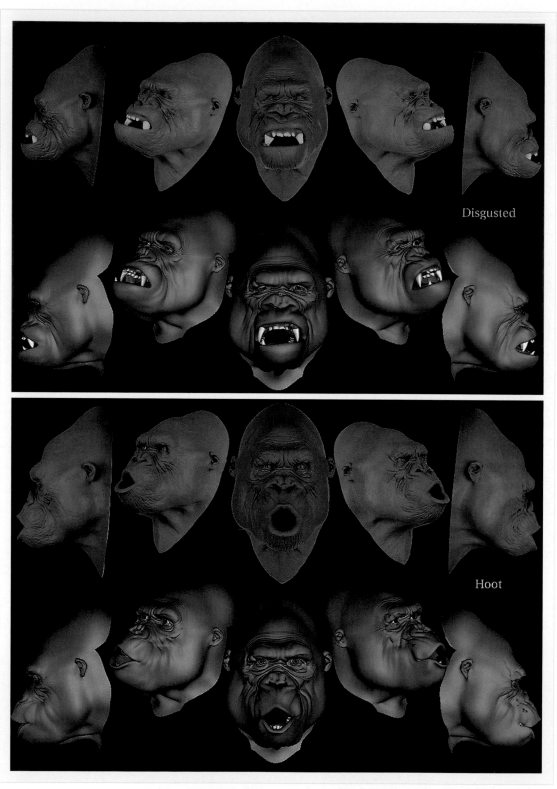

Disgusted

Hoot

Top: Top shows various angles of clay sculpting from Weta Workshop of Kong's 'Disgusted' expression. Bottom of the shot is a test to make sure Kong's digital facial expressions match the Workshop sculpt. Below: Top shows various angles of clay sculpting from Weta Workshop of Kong's 'Hoot' expression. Bottom of the shot is a test to make sure Kong's digital facial expressions match the Workshop sculpt.

## HYENAS AROUND THE CARCASS

Other creatures are also developed further for reference purposes. Once a cast of each scannable maquette has been sent off for scanning into digital form, an extra cast is taken and airbrushed for two weeks or so by a team of painters to match color schemes designed by Gino Acevedo, Weta's visual creature effects art director.

"Back in the old days," says Gino, "I would paint the maquette—kind of a guess of what Peter was looking for, after having meetings with him. Then he would come and look at it and say, 'Hmm, no, I think it should be green rather than blue.' So I'd basically have to start over again. But now, with the gift of Photoshop, I can do a bunch of different designs and save the maquette until Peter has actually approved something."

Gino's color designs involve further exploration into the nature and habitat of each creature: "The Lambeosaur is a herbivore, so he needs camouflage coloration, because the raptors and the V-Rexes eat [them]. For the swamp centipede I wanted to try to get the tails looking very translucent, but the body is a very hard crablike shell.

"I usually take photographs of the sculpture, and then take them into Photoshop and come up with a bunch of different designs for the coloring. Peter and Fran can pick one out, then I have my guys paint the maquette. So then we can bring that painted maquette over to Digital, and they can use that as reference for coloring the digital creatures."

And then, for Kong, there are hair studies. One thigh-high maquette of Kong on all fours has been completely covered with thousands of hairs, which took two and a half months to be added. And there's a maquette of Kong's head with extra details

Top: V-Rex matriarch ready for mold making. Middle: Paint study on the matriarch scannable maquette. Left: V-Rex open-mouth study

such as eyelashes. "This is a silicone head. It's all squishy," says Gino, poking at its nose to show how soft and pliable it is. "After it was painted, Dominee Till and her team punched in all the hair. It's yak hair, from different parts of the yak—the hair on the belly is thinner and finer, so we've used that around the muzzle. You grab one hair at a time and put it in a little hook, like a sewing needle that's been cut through the eye, and you push it into the silicone, and when you pull it out, the hair stays inside there. Depending on the angle that you punch the hair into it, it dictates the direction and the flow of it."

The hairy models are fantastic references for the digital effects team. Hair is complex because it moves so much. The team creating the digital Kong's hair can reference the hairy maquettes. They can feel the hair, lift the hair, and turn a fan on it to see how it might move in the wind.

Kong with hair is a different creature from the earlier, hairless versions. Suddenly all the effort that the designers and sculptors have put into giving Kong character and personality pays off. One can see his great age, his weariness, his suffering, and the loneliness and toughness of his existence.

"He's going through a few more changes right now," says Gino. "We found in animating Kong that the brow is too heavy. It's hard to get light in so you can see the eyes. So they're going to shift the brow back a little bit, make it a bit smaller."

Ben Wootten, head of design at Weta Workshop, has been working with the animation and creatures teams at Weta Digital, talking through how the creatures walk or why they're built in a certain way, and working to resolve creature design issues. "You'd like to think you've cracked it in a static sculpt," he says,

"but even if you've done twenty facial-expression studies, they're still not alive, they're still not animated, you're still not seeing them lit as they'll be lit in the film, so you don't know whether you're losing Kong's eyes under the shadows of his brow and his eyes need to be bigger, or whether the droopy eye is reading or not, or that the snaggle tooth is just too distracting and moves the lips too much when they're trying to get him to express. You don't really know how these things are going to work until you start seeing them come to life on the screen.

"At the end of the day, Kong has to be as viable a character as Denham or Jack or Ann. He's got to be as strong as Gollum, without dialogue. So the nuances of his design are extreme. He has to be perfect or else you won't buy into him. It's like deciding that you need to design Jack Black, and you build him from scratch to get an end result that is as original and subtle and varied as Jack Black is in real life—you can imagine how hard that would be. And that's what they're going through with Kong."

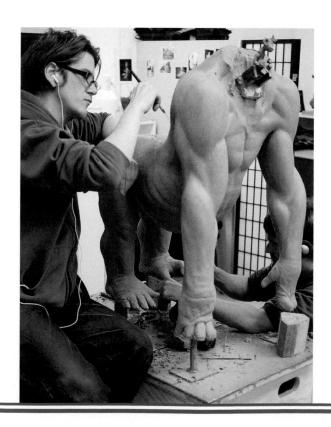

Right: Jamie Beswarick detailing a Kong maquette.
Opposite page: Andy Serkis poses with the head of Kong.

164

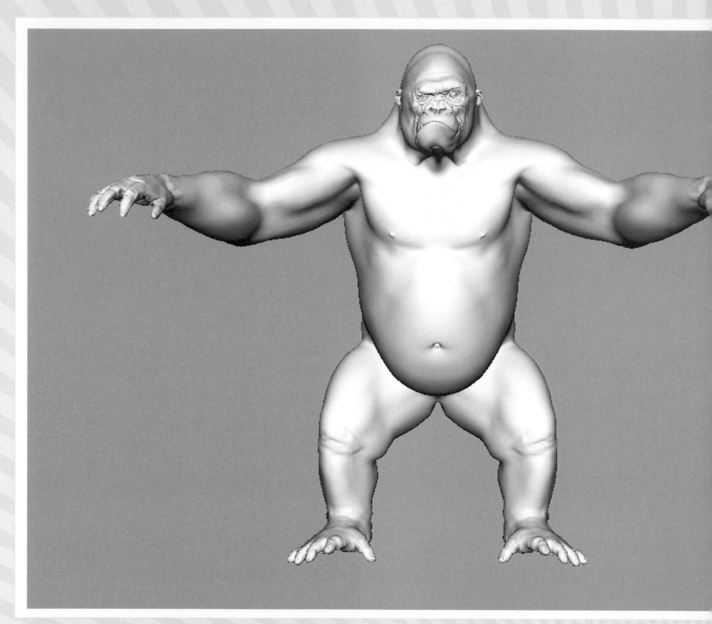

A nontextured, work-in-progress digital Kong model.

"There are more different types of creatures in *King Kong* than there are in the whole of *The Lord of the Rings* trilogy," says Weta Digital's Matt Aitken. "Modeling the creatures was a huge set of work to do in a very short space of time."

Matt is the pre-pro CG supervisor. "Obviously what we do here at Weta Digital is postproduction, since we take film off set and add visual effects to it," he says. "But within that, there's a preproduction and production aspect to it. The preproduction aspect is getting things ready for use in digital effects shots. There are thirty-seven people just doing digital modeling on this show."

Insects, birds, buildings, cars, planes, trees, boats, benches, even digital doubles of the actors—you name it, the modelers have made it. Or, if they haven't made it, they have tweaked it.

Matt has a 3D laser scan of Weta Workshop's model of Kong on his computer screen. "The models we get from the Workshop are a fantastic resource, but they're not the final word," he says. "With this guy, we don't want to lose his personality, but we're playing around with his head size, belly size, respective arm and leg lengths. Digital is a really good place to explore the design. If Peter said to make Kong's head five percent smaller, that's probably a four-week job on a clay sculpture, whereas on the computer it's a ten-minute job."

A dozen or so key creatures were first modeled in plasticine by Weta Workshop sculptors, but many more creatures were built from scratch by digital modelers. "When we were looking at the number of different creatures that we had to create for this show, it was a daunting prospect for Weta Workshop to do them all— their physical sculpts take months. So we're looking at new technologies, some of which we've already developed in-house, which enable us to model at very fine detail on the computer. We still like to get sculpts, because there's something real and organic about a creature that somebody's created by hand. But two-thirds of the creatures in the film have been entirely created in the computer from the Workshop's designs—including a giant-size weta!"

Among the creatures modeled digitally are some creepy-crawlies created for a scene that didn't make the cut in the original *King Kong*—the lost spider scene. "It was dropped because it was too horrific. Peter's put it back in," says Matt. "After the sailors all fall off the log, they fall down into the pit. In Peter's film, they think they've survived, but then they realize that they're not alone. These hordes of giant insects, pit-dwelling creatures, set on them and tear them apart."

For the film's juicier moments, such as sailors being munched or crunched to

## DIGITAL MODELS

A nontextured giant weta digital model.

Digital pit spider scale test, using a generic digital double crewman.

death, the modelers have built digital doubles of more than twenty of the actors. Matt replaces the Kong on his screen with a model of a human head. It is a near-perfect replica of Colin Hanks, who plays Preston, detailed enough to see the texture of his skin.

"We've got a new face scanner which can create a 3D model like this in two seconds. We scan the actors doing a whole lot of different expressions." He finds a scan of actor Andy Serkis as Lumpy the cook, with his face stretched wide in apparent horror. "We can use this for the really dramatic shots, where maybe he's being thrown around by one of those pit creatures. There may be just a moment or two where you get a clear look at his face."

If necessary, the faces of the digital doubles can be animated: "We're doing Ann with what I call the Gollum system, where we build a full animation system for her. We've even got a set of tools that groom her hair. It's like hairstyling."

"Creating realistic digital doubles involves many of Weta Digital's pre-production departments," says Eileen Moran, visual effects producer.

"We start with models, textures, and shaders, and then move on to creatures for the cloth and hair simulations. Because we have so many digital doubles, including hero doubles of the principal cast, it is crucial that they are indistinguishable from the actors."

Matt credits *The Lord of the Rings* for providing the resources to build Weta Digital into a cutting-edge visual effects facility. "With *Kong*," he says, "we're taking things to the next level. We can't use the technology that we used on the last show—it's never good enough. It's such a constantly moving field that we're forever having to reinvent the way we do things to stay one step ahead of the audience. In twenty years' time, audiences will see the holes in today's technology. But with Kong, like Gollum from *The Lord of the Rings*—those key scenes where he's arguing with himself—I like to think audiences will still be enjoying those. I think the best work that we do will have a timeless quality about it—not because of the technology, but because of the artistry."

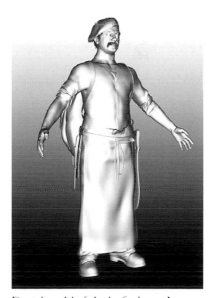

Digital model of Andy Serkis as Lumpy.

Clockwise: Early V-Rex scale test. V-Rex matriarch skeleton rig. V-Rex matriarch muscle rig. V-Rex juvenile muscle test.

The creatures department at Weta Digital, illuminated by the soft glow of many computer screens, is quietly humming with activity. Dana Peters, creature supervisor, is putting a brontosaurus through its paces.

"The creatures department is all about making things movable," he says, as the digital dinosaur does the Brontosaur equivalent of star jumps.

He rummages through his computer files and a V-Rex leaps onto the screen. It looks just as Weta Workshop sculptors created it—a colorless creature with finely detailed surface features, such as claws and wrinkles. "This is what we get from the models department—just a hollow, stationary, three-dimensional shell. We put the equivalent of bones and joints inside it, based on what we guess the anatomy would be of a creature like this. Then, if the animators grab one of these leg controls, they can move the leg around wherever they want to, and the structures we've bound to those bones will move with it. Basically, we get the model and make it into a puppet."

That, apparently, is the easy part. The puppets are handed over to animators, who work out exactly what movements they will do for each shot. The animations are then sent back to the creatures department so the creatures can be fleshed out and beefed up with muscles.

## CREATURE CALISTHENICS

Dana clicks away the skin of the V-Rex, exposing the animal's muscles. "We build the skeleton, which is never ever going to be seen by anybody, but we build it anyway so we can attach our muscles," he says. "This is the hard part: we model all those muscles and define how they move and what they're joined to, so when the elbow rises the bicep flexes correctly."

He whisks away the mass of interconnected muscles and replaces it with a V-Rex clothed in skin, running in empty space. "See the effect of those muscles on the skin?" He points to a fold of skin beneath one hip. As the leg extends, the skin stretches beyond what should be its natural limit. It looks truly painful. "This area is difficult, between the hip and the belly," says Dana. "You have to decide whether you want the skin to stretch, or how much you want it to roll over the surface of the muscles. So we watch the creatures do some calisthenics and exercises. We're trying to get the way the muscle flexes as the leg straightens, and we're working on flattening and pulling those wrinkles out as the leg stretches forward and then having them wrinkle up a little bit more when it comes back."

The next step is to get the skin sliding over muscle and bone. "This is one of the latest capabilities that we didn't have in

*The Lord of the Rings*," says Dana. He brings up a raptor on his screen. "See its rib cage? We want to get the skin sliding over that rib cage. Traditionally, the skinning attaches itself—you can tell particular points on the skin to pay attention to certain muscles underneath it. The difficult part is getting it to slide over the muscles a bit, instead of following them exactly. It's the little details that make it more realistic.

"The next thing is to try to add some dynamics into the muscles." He points out the hips and the back of the tail on the V-Rex. As the creature's foot stomps down on virtual ground, the muscles and skin of the hip and tail ripple, as if resonating from the impact. "That adds to the sense of weight and scale. Right when it hits, if it jiggles a bit, you feel like the muscles are moving. . . . We're doing everything we can to make these creatures look massive and powerful."

The animators, meanwhile, are working with simpler muscleless puppets. Once they have choreographed a creature's movement for a shot, the creatures department will add its dynamic, interconnected skin and muscles. "We have it set up so we can just insert a file and it does all this stuff automatically," says Dana. "But we do run into problems. For example, Kong might raise his arm more than we expected in one shot, so we might have to go in and massage his muscles."

That seems fair—a nice massage after putting the creatures through all that exercise.

Opposite page: Final shot of a V-Rex in the film. This page, top: Digital V-Rex bull model. Below: A lighting occlusion wedge.

Rigid Geo for Kong animation.

Animation director Eric Leighton would crawl inside his computer if he could. He snatches at the little gray representation of Kong currently on his screen: "I want to just get in there and grab that guy and move him around!" He laughs.

Eric, animation director Christian Rivers, and a team of fifty animators are responsible for bringing myriad creatures in *King Kong* to life—"primarily Kong, the star of the show," says Eric, "but it's a Peter Jackson movie, so there are lots and lots of monsters, lots of dinosaurs, lots of action, and we're responsible for the performances on all those guys."

The Kong on Eric's screen is a far cry from the fleshed-out, furry version audiences will see on the big screen. This little Kong is represented by a series of cylinders in shades of gray. "A representation of the volume of everything on the character has been attached to his skeleton," says Eric. "In other words, you take a cylinder that is roughly sculpted into the shape of his upper arm, and you attach it to his upper arm bone. Each of these little slices around his torso is attached to one of the vertebrae on his spine. So when you animate the bones, the bones then drive this 3D representation of bits of his body. But this is just for animation. And the only reason we do this in animation is speed. We can move this guy around very fast."

Animating any version of Kong more complex than this hollow collection of cylinders would be laboriously slow. "You'd have to move his arm a bit and then wait a minute," says Eric. For this reason, the animators are happiest when working with the simplest of puppets. "For all the really good animators that I've worked with, the faster they work, the better the work is, because . . . they're feeling the flow and the motion and the performance."

Despite not being able to physically take hold of the Kong on his screen, Eric considers digital animation to be much like the stop-motion, frame-by-frame animation that Willis O'Brien used for the original *Kong*. The digital puppet can be posed in any position, just as a physical stop-motion character can be posed. "You put a lot of animation controls on the digital puppet, and then you can move it around, just like you can move an armature," Eric says. "To animate it, you would position it wherever you want it and basically take a 3D snapshot of that pose, which is called a key frame. Then you'd say, 'One second later I want this arm to be here,' so you'd move it and take a snapshot there. So then, in one second, you'll see it going in a straight line from here to here. But then you say, 'Okay, a half a second in, I want the hand to go here,' and you take another snapshot of that. Now when you scrub through that

# ANIMATION

same second, it will actually describe an arc. You end up putting thousands of key frames on every single shot on every joint."

Before the animators launch into the more bone-crunching, tooth-and-claw, action-packed moments in the movie, they take each creature for a quiet stroll. Animation supervisor Atsushi Sato has been testing walk cycles and exploring how creatures might run, swim, fly, or gallop.

"Each character has its own behavior and style of action," he says. "Before we start production shots, we need to define the character—how fast it moves, how big its stride is, what its wing cycle should be. We have many types of characters—insects, bats, also digital doubles that stand in for humans. Animating humans is difficult. People know how they move, so you have to make it quite realistic."

Scale is an especially significant factor in defining the movement style of the larger creatures. "Why do people like dinosaurs? Because they are huge," says Atsushi. "We have to make them look big. But we also want them to be quite active and fast. If we animate the character too fast, it will make it look smaller. We have to find the point that it moves fast but still looks huge."

An impression of enormous weight can be given by having relatively large areas of a creature's body affected by each move. "When a dinosaur turns his head," says Atsushi, "if we move just his head, it looks light. If we make his shoulders follow through as the head turns, that's the thing that makes the character look heavy."

The animators have been working on movement styles for Kong himself for months. "Right now we are changing Kong's concept a little bit," says Atsushi. "He started out more like a monster type, but now we are moving into more naturalistic gorilla-like movement, in terms of facial expression and behavior."

Many hours' worth of documentary footage on

Different stages of the raptor's run cycle.

A raptor motion test.

176

gorillas has given the animators a wealth of reference material, but not all of Kong's movement styles can be based on the actions and behavior of real gorillas as caught on film. "We have footage of gorillas quite agitated. They threaten, they intimidate others to protect the group, but they don't really fight for life," says Atsushi. "They are kind of hitting each other, but they're just playing."

"It's an exaggerated reality," says Eric, "so we want the power and believability underneath, but then we want to entertain on top. So we're making them all characters—not just Kong but the dinosaurs as well. We're quite a bit more active with using tails as a performance device on the dinosaurs. They're predatory and they . . . start sweeping around and getting excited about stuff," he says, slapping and swishing his arm heavily on the tabletop, "which we wouldn't do on a naturalistic documentary-type film. It is characterizing on top of the reality of what they are.

"There's a lot of fighting in this movie and Kong punches a lot of dinosaurs. That punch, when he hits their head, it takes a long time for that wave of momentum to go all the way through their body to the end of their tail. It's not like human scale where you punch them and they just go down. You punch that dinosaur and . . ." Eric sends a slow, exaggerated wave of motion rippling down his own body, from head to tail-

bone. "Any tricks like that to show scale. It's reality-based. We do want that stuff to feel as real as possible, but they have to play huge. I think everything in this movie is huge. Kong is huge, the dinosaurs are huge, the trees are huge, the rocks are huge, the ferns are huge—everything is huge!" He laughs.

"All that motion then transfers over onto a beastie with skin, and there's a whole muscle system that goes inside of him . . . if I stop like this"—he slams his fist down on the desk—"you see there's a shake on my biceps. Hopefully once the muscle model is working, some of that stuff will be 'automatic.' I don't want to hand-animate that on every muscle  it would be insane, we'd need six years! So we'll automate as much as possible. But if I want to communicate tension by having the tendons standing out in the neck, that's a performance issue and I would have to hand key-frame that. There are lots of little details like that that we need to key frame."

Most scenes have been roughed out in advance by the previz team, giving the animators a clear guide to what a creature needs to be doing in any given shot. "Previz is . . . visual storytelling, brainstorming, coming up with gags and different ideas," says Eric. "It's working on how the characters interact with each other. All the rough performances and general timing and positioning are worked out at the previz stage. But then we take that and make it bigger on each step of the path."

In fine-tuning a character as complex as Kong, the animators face a multitude of choices and performance issues. "We're playing Kong's performance very animal," says Christian Rivers. "And I don't mean just that he's running around on all fours like a gorilla. As an animal, he's always in the now. An ani-

Animation shows Kong swinging on vines as he fights a V-Rex.

177

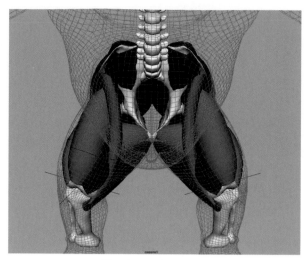

Kong's muscle system.

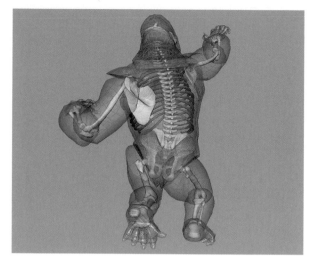

A Kong animation skeleton rig.

178

mal doesn't really know when it's dying. They know when they're wounded and they react instantaneously to the pain, and they'll carry a limb if it's hurt, but they won't sit there and mope about the fact that they're in pain."

The animators have chosen to pull back from overly expressive facial animation for Kong. "We're trying to make his performance very subtle and keep him very enigmatic," says Christian, who believes that Kong's lack of sentimentality about his situation will allow audience members to respond to him with their own emotions.

"It's something that worked very well in the previz. We chose not to include any facial animation and keep this rather blank character face of Kong. But the Empire State Building sequence where he dies packed a huge emotional punch with everyone who watched it. Kong wasn't investing in his own demise. He was just an animal that was being killed and was trying to protect Ann."

Christian has been working with actor Andy Serkis on the motion capture stage, where Andy is further developing the character aspects of Kong's performance. "Andy's an amazing actor and he's studied gorillas inside out," says Christian. "I talk

about the specifics of the shot as far as the action that Kong needs to be doing, but Andy's totally looking into the motivations and getting under the skin of what Kong is and why he's doing it."

Andy's performances as Kong can be captured on computer and used instead of key-frame animation to drive the digital Kong for many scenes, but not without some tweaking. "The only way to really turn Andy into Kong is to augment his performance. Once it's in the computer you digitally alter his physiology. So certain steps that Andy may take with his legs would need to be made shorter. The amount of weight that he puts on his arms when he comes down on his hands . . . we'd need to add animation into the shoulders. It's basically embellishing it, but still using all Andy's performance choices that he made on the day."

But for many action-packed moments, such as the battle between Kong and the V-Rexes, Kong's animation will most likely be key-framed. "You can get some fantastic results both ways," says Christian. "Where Andy's performance has become invaluable is anything where there's a connection with Ann."

Meanwhile, Eric can sometimes be found on all

fours on the set, helping to ensure that the live action fits in with the digital action in visual effects shots. "I've been lucky enough to get on set quite a bit . . . working with the stunties and actors to tell them where the invisible dinosaurs are and where the invisible giant monkey is and where they need to look. We just did a sequence with Adrien Brody on set which was really fun. To just run around and throw myself on the ground and pretend I'm twenty-five feet tall, slamming my fists in anger and all that, it's a really great experience." Eric laughs. "And often we come up with ideas on set. If you're working with the actors or the stunties, they'll say, 'Oh, that's cool,

but what if I do this as well.' Every step of the way, more excitement and energy gets put into it.

"It's constantly evolving here—lots of creativity at every level," says Eric. "That's the way that Peter Jackson works. It's the best and worst of working for him. The worst part is that you can never be sure of anything. You can bleed on something and love it and love it, and then all of a sudden it's gone. It's hard sometimes to let go, but you know it's always making the movie better. The best part is, Peter really, really fosters creative input from everybody on the crew. And ultimately when you see the final product, you feel a part of yourself in it."

Final shot of Kong confronting his foe.

Video capture from *Peter Jackson's King Kong: The Official Game of the Movie.*

While *King Kong*, the movie, was in pre-production, so too was the video game: *Peter Jackson's King Kong*. Peter, a fan of video games, handpicked Ubisoft to create the game and worked closely with the game's developers to ensure that it had the look and feel of the movie.

The video game is set primarily on Skull Island, although it ends in New York City. The player initially plays as Jack Driscoll, battling the deadly perils of the jungle to find and save Ann, but at certain points in the game is given opportunities to play as Kong. "It's all about reliving the emotions of the movie," says the game's creator, Michel Ancel. "You go from this little human, fighting to survive, to being the mighty and powerful Kong."

Weta Workshop provided Ubisoft with Skull Island concept art, so the game's designers have created 3D interactive environments based on the same artwork used by the set and miniature builders. Weta Digital supplied digital doubles of the actors and 3D digital models of the creatures, which the Ubisoft team have adapted and reinterpreted to fit the constraints of the game engine, thereby maintaining the look and feel of these characters and creatures.

The concept designers at Weta Workshop did many creature designs that could not fit into the movie, and the game, with a playing time of more than fifteen hours, proved to be an ideal home for them.

Screenwriter Philippa Boyens worked with the development team to come up with new scenes and dialogue unique to the game. One new scene occurs almost as soon as the game begins. "In a game, you always need to start with a very impressive and action-packed sequence, to make sure to hook the gamer from the beginning," says Michel. "So whereas in the movie, when the crew arrives on Skull Island, it's all about exploring and pretty calm, in the game they are attacked right away on the beach by giant crabs."

An unusual feature of the game is that there is no heads-up display to indicate the player's health and weapons status. This is to make the game a more immersive experience for the player, so that it is less like playing a game and more like participating in the movie.

"The atmosphere of the game is extremely cinematic, so much that even when someone else is playing, you can watch and get engrossed in the action on the screen," says Michel. "But our main objective was to make a game: it is even more fun to play it!"

## PETER JACKSON'S KING KONG:
### THE OFFICIAL GAME OF THE MOVIE

Shot of the Brontosaur stampede sequence from the final film.

Lumpy the cook is running for his life. He has a tommy gun clasped in one hand, a bulky pack bouncing on his back, a cigar clenched between his teeth, and a look on his face suggesting that any moment now he will be dead meat. But for all his desperate effort, he is getting nowhere.

The scene is the Brontosaur stampede, in which herds of digital Brontosaurs and raptors will eventually charge down an endless gorge, trampling and snapping at the fleeing sailors. But for now, the scenery is pure green screen. Andy Serkis as Lumpy is running and stumbling helter-skelter on a speeding treadmill. He is dressed as Lumpy, he looks as terrified as Lumpy, but the object of his terror is yet to be added to the scene. Standing in for the belly of the Brontosaur running over him are two stuntmen batting at him with a bundle of green-screened padding on a long green pole.

"We use this type of simple interaction to get some contact between the digital and live-action characters," says Eric Saindon, digital effects supervisor for the Skull Island sequences. "We get a lot of guys running with wires holding them up—Adrien or Jack with wires hooked onto their waistline, and then running on a green screen, not going anywhere, just the camera moving around. They're pretty funny to see, and they're all running at different speeds!" Eric laughs. "You usually

## THE STAMPEDE

don't see their feet hit the ground, so we can speed them up if we need to. They said Andy Serkis ran the fastest."

The gorge itself has been built in miniature, and the miniatures unit has been filming a variety of fast-moving shots racing down the gorge, as a backdrop for the actions of the human and digital characters. The dinosaur action, meanwhile, is in the hands of the animators. It is up to Eric Saindon's team to bring all the elements of the scene together.

The live-action shot of each actor is converted into a kind of digital postcard that can be stuck into the scene in an appropriate position relative to the gorge and the dinosaurs, then moved along to keep pace with or be overtaken by the rampaging monsters. "We take the . . . cards and move those through the scene," says Eric, "as if they were running at the speed that the camera is moving down through the shot, and maybe they're [running] in between the legs of the bronto."

CG supervisor Simon Clutterbuck and Frank Reuter, 2D lead, are working on shadows that have digitally been painted over the actors in the scene. "They're underneath the brontos, so we're having to animate the shading as if they're being shadowed by the creatures," Eric explains. But that's not all the CG artists will do to the actors. Some shots

191

require the amputation of a limb or two. "At the point where the actor can no longer do what we need the character to do, it becomes a CG character," says Eric. "We fade between the two over five or ten frames, so hopefully most people won't see it. Just when this actor is about to get squished, the anima-

tors start animating the double, and then they can do whatever they want to it."

In other words, Andy and company may get batted and shaken around a fair bit, but no actors have been trampled or eaten during the making of this movie.

Shot from the miniature of the Brontosaur stampede.

Shot from the live-action Brontosaur stampede.

Lit and rendered Brontosaurs.

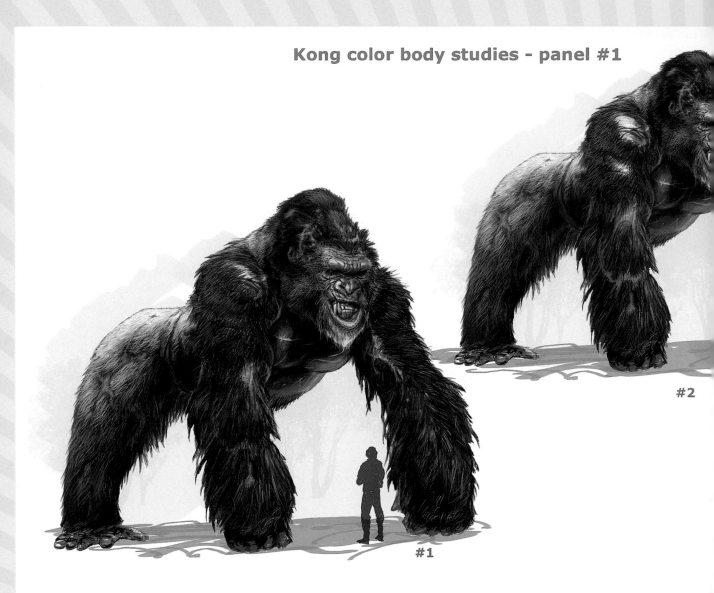

**Kong color body studies - panel #1**

#2

#1

Kong sketches showing scale.

"When the original *King Kong* was made in 1933, people knew very little about gorillas," says Andy Serkis, the actor charged with shaping Kong's latest performance. "People thought of them as demonic beasts."

Mountain gorillas were discovered in Rwanda by Captain Robert von Beringe, a German explorer, in 1902. He immediately shot one and shipped it back to a Berlin museum. The public imagination ran wild.

"The 1933 version of Kong was sort of a gorilla," says Andy, "but he stands up and walks around and beats his chest, which very much fits in with early explorers' and hunters' perceptions of this half-man, half-beast."

Nowadays, audiences are more enlightened as far as gorillas are concerned. Since the 1950s, decades of meticulous research, most notably by *Gorillas in the Mist* zoologist Dian Fossey, have debunked the myth of savage man-beasts and revealed gorillas to be peaceful, family-oriented creatures, although given to occasional displays of aggression.

For the 2005 movie and a contemporary audience, Andy is adamant that Kong should be as much a gorilla as he can make him: "We'll earn the audience's belief in the character if we honor the truthfulness of gorilla behavior as much as we can."

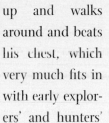

# THE 8TH WONDER OF THE WORLD

That belief drove Andy on a personal quest to observe gorillas in the wild: "I watched hundreds of hours of video footage, but there's nothing like spending time with gorillas to get inside how they operate."

First, Andy spent two months working with keepers at London Zoo and formed a particular attachment to a female gorilla called Zaire. "We kind of clicked as soon as we met. It's hard to explain to anyone who hasn't connected with a gorilla." He laughs. "Whenever she saw me come in, she'd rush up and bang the cage, and we'd play games. We spent a lot of time together, much to the chagrin of the young male silverback.

"You start from a very wide perspective of seeing them as a species, but you end up very quickly seeing them as individuals, which was a great lesson for me Kong isn't representing gorillas, he is a particular gorilla and has individual foibles and characteristics and moods. He's as idiosyncratic as any human being."

Just before the start of principal photography, Andy traveled to Rwanda in search of some of the world's last remaining mountain gorillas. There he hooked up with the Dian Fossey Gorilla Fund International, an organization dedicated to researching and protecting the endangered

orkshop

KONG
or body study

s Hunter

A silverback gorilla from Rwanda.

Andy Serkis studied silverbacks in order to
mimic their movements.

species. For more than a week he went out every day
with trackers, following one of several groups of gorillas closely monitored by the DFGFI.

"All the gorillas can be recognized by their individual nose prints and personalities. You have a responsibility to keep a five-meter distance from them,
but you can be completely surrounded and they'll
come up to you and barge into you and knock you
over. You just have to defer if you're in the way of a
silverback and he's about to charge—which they do!

"It was the most extraordinary, mesmerizing,
and unforgettable experience," Andy remembers. "It's
like watching a big family. You see the patriarch, and
the women with babies on their breasts, and the kids
fighting. But it's very peaceful. They live in this huge
salad bowl. They've got food all around them, so a lot
of their day is quite relaxing. They eat, they sleep,

then the silverback gets up and signals to the rest of
the group and they move off. And they talk to each
other: they're all grunting and saying, 'I'm all right,
are you okay?' They sing and they laugh.

"And then, suddenly, a helicopter flew over very
low to the ground, and you could see terror, and
these beautiful, slow-moving, graceful creatures suddenly panicking and freezing."

That terror-charged scene gave Andy an opening
into understanding Kong's behavior in New York:
"He's an animal that's been transported out of his
own environment into a very alien situation. When
he breaks out of the theater, he's not an out-of-control
beast that goes out of his way to kill and smash and
cause terror. He's like a rabbit caught in headlights.
He's backing into things and smashing things—
rather like when that helicopter came low."

The movie has a fantastical element: Kong is twenty-five feet tall; he fights dinosaurs. So, how much of the gorilla behavior that Andy had observed could possibly be applicable to the film?

"I think Pete really wants the iconic imagery of Kong beating his chest with his fists. In reality, gorillas use cupped hands, and it's very rapid. The chest-beating display starts with a hoot, hoot, hoot, and then it goes into a shriek and a kind of a roar as they stand up. They use their whole bodies to get up off the ground, but they can't stay up for too long, they fall back down again. It's often accompanied by side-to-side movement and charges and back and forth. It doesn't really work as a static thing. That is the one place where artistic license is probably applicable.

"Gorillas are wild animals. They display and attack if they feel threatened. On the whole they are peaceful creatures, but Kong, through most of this film, is under attack, either from dinosaurs or from men. At times his desire is to attack Jack, but he's not railing against humankind. He just wants to find the other male that's threatened him.

"We're not aiming to humanize him. We can't express his emotions in a human way. You don't really know what a gorilla's thinking. A lot of the intention is carried in the eyes, and they avert their gaze a lot.

"Their timing is offbeat, it's not human timing. Two actors playing a love scene look into each other's eyes. Kong is a gorilla, so he might express it differently. He might not look at Ann, but he might open his hand to her. As a human being you will read the emotion, so we're intending to let the audience do some of the work. We're making dramatic decisions, but we're experimenting with using real gorilla behavior to provide that tension.

"We keep revisiting footage and looking at behavior, every day. It's complete gorilla world here at the moment!"

189

Top: Conceptual art by Gus Hunter, showing Kong being revealed to the helpless Ann through the haze and smoke of the fiery wall.
Bottom: Naomi Watts as Ann Darrow, seeing Kong for the first time.

"Kong is a silverback gorilla who's past his prime. He's battle-scarred, weary, lonely, haunted, and slightly crazed.

"He's the last of his species. He was once part of a social group, but now he's devoid of any contact except for anything that wants to kill him. He's an alpha male, and every day's a struggle for survival. He's very toughened. But, within that, there's a small chink in his soul that has an innocence that harks back to being a social creature. His desire, his driving force, is to have companionship—which is why he becomes a tragic figure.

# A TRAGIC TALE

## AS TOLD BY ANDY SERKIS

"The first time you see him, you see this ferocious, hugely violent beast crashing out of nowhere, and it assaults your senses, rather like a silverback attack. It's terrifying! It's almost harking back to the 1930s perception of gorillas. But in the end you learn there's more to him.

"There's a place where Kong takes the human sacrifices to and kills them. They're terrified and he almost can't bear the screaming. He doesn't eat them, just kills. It's a frustration that he has with them.

"But Ann takes him by surprise. He's about to kill her, but she trips over by mistake, and he's a bit shocked by that. She senses that. She throws herself down again and builds up into her vaudeville routine. And he's curious about it and becomes engrossed. What he really likes is her falling over.

"In the end, she's exhausted, can't do it anymore. He throws this huge display of rage. He's got his fist hovering over her, to pulverize her, but there's something in him that can't do it. He has connected with this being in a way that he's not done since he was cradled by his mum. And at that moment, she's disempowered him. He backs off and lopes into the forest.

"Then he hears her scream. He powers over and again has this huge display in front of her. He wants to prove, to demonstrate, that he's the boss. It's a fight to the death with the V-Rexes and he's triumphant! He's doing it for her.

"In the face-off between Kong and the V-Rex, Ann makes a decision to primp for Kong. It's like a pub fight over a girl. His testosterone levels shoot through the roof when he knows that she's gone for him and that she needs him. He just powers in. And then he walks off.

"He left her the first time because she's broken him. This time he's just demonstrated his power. He walks away and she runs after him. From that point their relationship has equilibrium. They've bonded."

Naomi Watts and Adrien Brody share a dramatic moment.

Kong's lair is an island of broken rock surrounded by floor-to-ceiling blue screens and a clutter of filmmaking paraphernalia. Naomi Watts, as Ann Darrow, lies as if asleep in a nest of padded blue blocks representing Kong's hand. Behind her, a twisted mass of roots, vines, grasses, moss, and dark rock winds its way up to the lighting grid. On a ledge just above her is an immense skull, standing in for Kong's head. It has been borrowed from the skeleton of one of Kong's ancestors—a scattering of enormous ribs, knucklebones, and femurs on another rocky set, for now pushed aside behind the coffee urns and snack table at the far end of the soundstage.

Adrien Brody, as Jack Driscoll, is scheduled to sneak into the lair all day.

"Playback!" orders the first assistant director.

Music fills the warehouse—"Braveheart: Revenge." It has an urgent beat and a tone of energized suspense. The amplified sound of slow, heavy breathing crashes over it, like waves hitting a rocky shore.

"And . . . action!"

Adrien creeps over a tangle of thick roots and straw, shrinks against an outcrop of rock as he skirts past two blue poles representing Kong's outflung arm, and inches toward Naomi. "Ann!" he whispers. "Ann!" She opens her eyes, sees him.

# ON SET WITH KONG

Slowly, slowly, they reach out to each other, fingertips almost touching . . .

"Eyes!" calls director Peter Jackson.

Their eyes fly to the skull. The heavy breathing changes to a surprised grunt.

"And up!"

Naomi jolts her body as if suddenly snatched upward. Adrien stumbles back.

"And cut!"

Naomi and Adrien drop out of character. The music and grunts cease. Actor Andy Serkis, the source of Kong's heavy breathing, climbs down from his perch atop an A-frame ladder half-hidden in a forest of fans, tripods, and lighting stands. He fishes a set of false gorilla teeth out of his mouth and settles down to write some notes on a laptop computer.

Three actors are playing this scene, but only two of them can be physically present on the set. Kong will be added by Weta Digital later in postproduction. In a few weeks' time, Andy will start driving the digital Kong's performance through the magic of motion capture. For now, though, he is sidelined. He is simply too small to stand in for the twenty-five-foot gorilla.

"I've been his thumb," he points out.

A crew member walks past with his arm completely encased in a huge blue finger. In the shadows, behind trolleyloads of camera equipment, another crew member is wrapping a pole with foam and blue

A crew member holds up Kong's "finger" on set.

fabric. Both digits will be used to prod and thwack Naomi or her stunt double in the days to come.

"We use everything we can think of to give a sense of Kong's presence: sound, height, creating parts of him physically," says Andy. "I've picked Naomi up and walked her and put her down. I've been Kong's fist squeezing her, so she can physically hold on to me and feel like she's being squeezed by Kong's hand. And I'm doing the breathing and his vocalizations."

Enter the Kongalizer, a piece of software magicked up by postproduction sound wizard Chris Ward and hooked up to the set-side sound system. Andy puts in his fake teeth, cups his hands over his mouth, and makes animal noises into a microphone, feeding every breath, growl, and throat rattle to the Kongalizer, which distorts and reverbs the sounds in such a way that, when amplified, they sound like the cavernous vocalizations of an enormous beast. Simply put, Andy's voice goes into the Kongalizer and comes out as the voice of Kong.

"It's a way of evoking Kong spatially, and giving him size," says Andy. More than the giant blue fingers and ancestral skull, his Kongalized voice creates a sense of Kong's presence for the other actors: he is living, he is breathing, he is huge, and he is right here in his lair.

"Sometimes," says Andy, "I'll actually speak

Andy Serkis participated on set in a number of ways, including holding Naomi Watts, to give a sense of Kong's physical presence.

Kong's subtext or physicalize his actions: 'Kong is rising, he's rising up. He's beating his chest . . .' Then the cameras know to lift up too. I'll be emoting as Kong but calling out as myself: 'And now I'm smashing Jack! I'm smashing him with my left fist! And now I'm stomping him! I'm rising up! I'm beating my chest!' That energizes the scene."

Adrien creeps into Kong's lair again, but now the cameras are close on Naomi.

Peter Jackson guesses the *Braveheart* theme isn't working for her: "Do you want some emotional music? 'Reaching for the Moon,' would that work for you?"

Sound recordist Hammond Peek cues up the song from a library of tracks chosen by screenwriters Fran Walsh and Philippa Boyens: "Mozart," "Al Jolson," "Drumming," and "Hollow Log Music," among others.

"We started playing in music at the green-screen stage," Hammond explains. "A large part of my job is to create atmosphere for the actors. Not much of the sound we record is usable."

That's not because he is bad at his job. The huge fans used to give Skull Island a windswept look make quite a racket. Many of the filming venues are warehouses with thin brick walls, construction sites next door, planes overhead, and rain on their tin roofs. For most scenes, the actors will return during postproduction to rerecord their dialogue. The dialogue

Hammond records on set will primarily serve as a guide track.

"Playback!"

Andy breathes. The smooth voice of Ella Fitzgerald croons out:

*The moon and you appear to be*
*So near and yet so far from me . . .*

"Ann! Ann!" Adrien and Naomi reach out to each other. Naomi's eyes fill with tears. The wind whips at her face.

"Cut! That one was a bit blinky," calls Peter from his comfy sofa, where he sits with Fran and Philippa, watching a set of monitors receiving video feeds from the cameras.

Naomi wipes the tears away. The cameras roll again. She sees Adrien and her eyes mist over. She doesn't blink. She reaches out to him . . . so near and yet so far.

"Eyes! And up! And cut!"

"I loved the way you allowed yourself a slight smile at Jack," Peter says to Naomi.

"Naomi's an actress who's very much used to playing off every moment and receiving what another actor does," notes Andy . . . which is all very well for developing the Ann/Jack romance,

Andy Serkis gives Naomi Watts a focal point for her interactions with Kong.

but what of the relationship between Ann and Kong?

Whenever possible, Andy has placed himself where Kong's head will be: "I can be twenty, forty feet away, up on top of a scissor lift. But it's very important, although we can't physically touch each other, that we're inside each other's head space and that it gives her something that is real, living, and playing acting decisions with her, so she doesn't have to just look up, pretend that someone's there, and drive her own emotions. She can respond to what I'm doing."

"Thank goodness for Andy," says Naomi. "He can really transport me to a whole other place. I'm not looking at him wearing a funny suit. I'm looking at him with all this behavior and all this feeling, and I can't imagine who else could make me feel the way he's making me feel. It's really something."

For Andy, however, this is just the first stage of creating Kong. Once principal photography wraps, he'll launch into months of motion-capture work, creating the performance that will drive the digital version of Kong. Naomi won't be there; she's way too big to interact physically with an Andy-sized Kong.

Which is why Andy's work on set is as much for Kong as it is for Ann: "Having lived through the scenes with Naomi, when I come to play them on my own without anybody there for nine weeks, I will have encoded into my muscles and my brain what each scene is about.

"There are so many different departments, all looking at their own particular thing: the survey department looking at the landscape, the camera department looking at the shots. With no actual Kong on set, it would be easy to lose sight of his performance. My job is to be the guardian of the character through the entire process."

# Going Ape

Andy Serkis wears a black gorilla suit when he plays Kong on set. "It's his wardrobe," says first assistant director Carolynne Cunningham. "He has a set of gorilla hands, and he has this gorilla body thing which Howard Berger from KNB Effects loaned us, and he's got this head like a gorilla's head. And it really transforms him and it makes a lot of difference. It makes you perceive him more as a gorilla than an actor playing a gorilla.

"The first time it came out, we all laughed, but after that we kind of got the point. I used to take him for walks in his little suit. He'd grab my hand. It was hysterical."

To many of his fellow actors, Andy appeared as Kong for the first time on the enormous Mount Crawford set—the gates to the jungle. Until then, most had only seen him playing his other role, Lumpy the cook.

"All of a sudden," recalls Colin Hanks, "he sort of pops up, and he starts going apeshit. And we're all in the moment, and he is freaking me out. I mean, he's a gorilla—albeit he's not a twenty-five-foot gorilla."

"I was so scared," says Jack Black. "He is so insane as King Kong. He is not a human. I was looking into the eyes of an insane beast!"

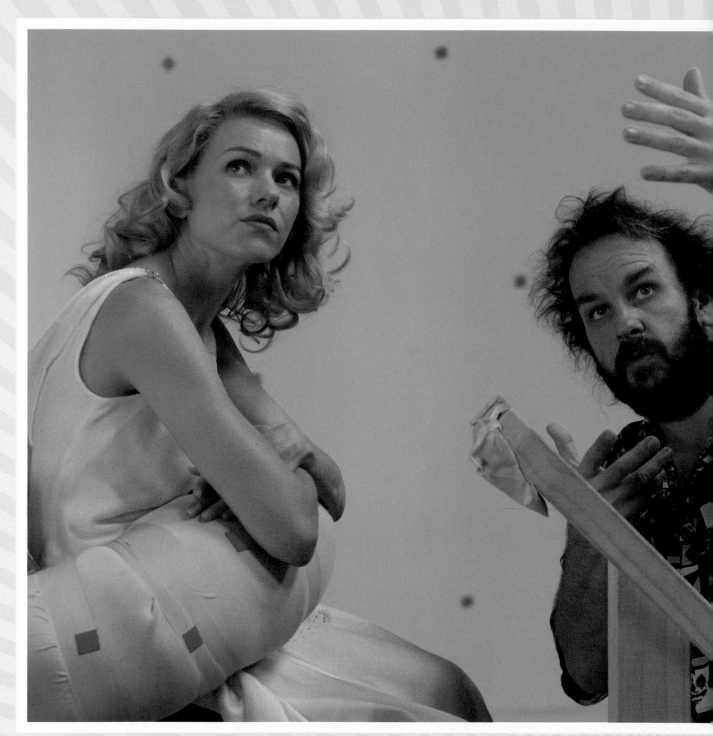

Peter Jackson gives Naomi Watts pointers as she sits in Kong's "grip."

For Naomi Watts, facing up to Kong was at first a daunting prospect. "Blue screen is a whole world that I'm not familiar with," says the actress. "It's the fear of the unknown."

In the last weeks of principal photography, she has been totally immersed in that world. Now that the scenes with sailors, Skull Island natives, and New York crowds are all in the can, attention has turned to the scenes between Ann Darrow and Kong. For days, Naomi has been sitting in a motion rig being poked and prodded by huge green or blue sausages wielded by the special effects team.

"It's a scary day when you come to set and you have grown men attacking you in bright green and blue suits," she says, laughing.

Eventually, the green or blue screens surrounding her will be digitally replaced by the streets of New York or vistas of Skull Island, and the sausages will be covered by the digital Kong's fingers. For now, though, the sausages, the motion rig, and Andy Serkis are all she has to work with.

"It's difficult," she says, "because you're looking up at this place, and Andy's up there in some big scissor lift, and you've got men in Lycra unitards who are being his thumb or some part of him, so you have to do whatever you can to get into zone and block out all these strange, bizarre things that are going on."

## IN SAFE HANDS

To represent the palm of Kong's hand, the special effects team has created a custom motion-rig seat that is a perfect fit for Naomi. "It's on a motion base," explains custom effects coordinator Steve Ingram. "It's a platform with a carbon-fiber and Kevlar molded seat. And on the back of that seat we've mounted a couple of Kong's fingers. They're covered in blue or green and can either be left hand or right hand. They come round and hold her in the seat. We can move it around all over the place . . . and get it into a position to match the previz of what she has to do in the shot."

That rig sure can move. At times it is like a bucking bronco or an amusement park ride. For the roughest moves, stunt double Min Windle takes Naomi's place. For the more distant shots, the Ann in Kong's hand is likely to be Naomi's digital double.

"Naomi will do the close-ups when you really need to see her face," says Steve. "And then Min will do the scary part, where the rig has to move really quickly and she's thrown around a lot, to a point where she is far enough away from camera to become a CG double."

Spotting Min's face in the finished film is likely to be tricky; the digital effects teams have plans to paste Naomi's face over it.

For some shots, such as the moment when Kong finds Jack in his lair and

Naomi Watts, against a green screen, in Kong's hand.

snatches Ann away, the transition from Naomi to Min to the digital Ann can occur within one apparently seamless shot. "It happens all the time," says Weta Digital's Eric Saindon. "It's a lot of morphing. If it's Naomi going to Min, then it would be a bit of a morph over a few frames. If you watched it frame by frame by frame, you might be able to catch a bit of a morph between the two. Hopefully you would never see that. And the same thing would happen if it went to a digital double. We would do a bit of a morph from Min or Naomi to our Ann digital double. She'll have the same hair and the same outfit and the same skin. All her textures are based on Naomi."

The morphing requires Min and Naomi to be dressed alike, with matching hair, and positioned as much as possible in the same place and at the same

angle at the moment of morphing. But with the motion rig vigorously thrashing them around, the digital team is not expecting an exact match. "Sometimes the digital paint department has to paint a few frames to merge between the two," says Eric. "Or maybe we'll wipe screen with a bat flying by and switch the two in between. All it takes is a frame."

Naomi loves the quieter moments between Ann and Kong. "Today's a really great scene that we're shooting," she says. "I'm trying to communicate with Kong and experience a moment and share it with him. You can't really talk to him, but you can try and use other ways to express and communicate. So it's really a beautiful moment where it's all about the eyes and the feelings, and the need to connect—we are two lost souls in this wild place, with the need for

Bonding with Kong.

companionship and the need to come together and trust each other."

In this respect, the movie diverges from the original, in which Ann was, for the most part, Kong's terrified captive. "There are so many great things that Peter and Fran and Philippa have done with the script that has made it so different," says Naomi. "Ann is much more modern, she's not screaming all the time, she's much more of a survivor. We're trying to be as authentic as we can with the period, but there are certain things that wouldn't translate for today's audiences if we were trying to match the first two movies."

Naomi met Fay Wray, the original Ann, before she died in 2004. "She gave me her blessing. I was nervous about that! I had seen both versions of *King Kong* before . . . [and] both actresses were great in the part. I didn't want to get too attached to the way they did things because otherwise you get into trying to imitate. I just tried to block it out of my head."

So here she is, surrounded by nothing but filmmakers and green screen, soaking in the imagined beauty of Skull Island or New York at dawn, and discovering some kind of bond with a not-yet-created Kong.

"So much of their relationship is really quite like any other relationship," she says. "He's ferocious, angry, but he's also loving. He takes care of her, he's protective. She's in this environment that is completely wild and dangerous, and she trusts him: I feel safe with you.

"He's the ultimate man. Don't you think?" Naomi laughs. "He is! Although he is perhaps lacking in social graces at times!"

Andy Serkis on the motion capture stage in a Kong mocap suit.

As principal photography wraps, New York is dismantled, costumes are boxed, and his fellow actors head back to their home countries, Andy Serkis is beginning nine weeks of grueling mocap (motion-capture) work.

In a big tin shed, just a stone's throw away from Weta Digital and Park Road Post, Andy is lying down, simulating Kong sleeping. One arm is outflung, one hand cradled gently at his chest. No rocky lair or jungle of roots and vines here: the set for today's scenes is a thick rubber mat, a couple of bare wooden risers, and a motley collection of benches and stools.

His leading lady is a disheveled Barbie doll. His costume is a blue-and-black, figure-hugging body-suit, bulked out by padded knees, elbows, gloves, and head-gear. A thick wad of foam padding rounds out his belly. Heavy weights are strapped to his arms, thighs, and ankles, to give his movements the momentum of a larger, heavier creature. In his mouth is a set of fake Kong teeth, and a microphone is taped to one cheek. He is dotted all over with silver spots.

Around and above him are dazzling pinpoints of light from many small spot-lights, each with a tiny camera next to it. Bundles of cables snake across the floor to a row of tables sporting a collection of lap-tops, keyboards, and monitors. One moni-tor shows footage of Adrien Brody as Jack,

# MOTION CAPTURE

creeping into Kong's lair. Another shows previz (previsualization animation) of Kong waking, setting Ann onto a ledge out of harm's way, and attacking Jack.

A third monitor shows a split-screen image of Andy and Kong. Both figures are in the low-resolution, blocky style of a pre-viz animation. They are digital puppets, one man-shaped, one gorilla-shaped, both imitating the real Andy. As Andy stands, so do the puppets.

It's all done with mirrors, says Matt Madden from Giant Studios, which owns the motion-capture tech-nology. He points to Andy's silver spots: "Those markers are placed on locations that best represent how his body is moving. The sil-very material is made up of a bunch of tiny little mirrors. It's the same material you see in street signs and running shoes. Our cameras have a light that shines down on those mirrors, the reflected light is shone back into the camera, the camera re-lays that information to the computer, and the computer does a 3D reconstruction in virtual space."

Andy leans forward and dangles his arms so that his knuckles rest on a low bench set up in front of him. The digital Andy puppet follows the move exactly, but the Kong puppet, with its longer arms, drops down onto all fours.

"The computer replica of Andy's body knows which of Andy's bones each marker

Andy Serkis physically acts out Kong's movements in conjunction with digital animation on screen behind him.

is on and where it is on that bone," says Matt. "Then we have the Kong character, which has different bone lengths. Our job is to define how Andy's motion should look on Kong and make that offset."

"The movements are one-to-one down as far as my waist," says Andy. "My legs are foreshortened on the Kong puppet, so they're really where my knees are. Getting used to locomotion like that is very weird."

The knee-high benches help. They have been strategically positioned as higher ground for Andy's hands, to allow him to move as if he too were on all fours. Foam cubes stand in for some rocks to be tossed aside, and foam squabs have been gaffer-taped to the benches at specific points he needs to thump, as Kong attempting to crush Jack.

Previz of the scene provides the mocap team with a clear guide to Kong's actions and the layout of his lair. During principal photography, survey cameras mapped the live-action sets so that they could be reproduced on computer. "We know exactly what the ground plan is that we're working to," says Andy, "and it's very, very precise."

Despite the detailed preplanning, there is still room for Andy to develop Kong's performance: "The other day, we were trying to find a way of Kong looking at Ann. It's a private moment, and he knows he feels connected to her. He was supposed to just have

her in his hand, and it's supposed to be quite a still scene. But eventually we found that a more physicalized version of the scene, where he starts to cradle her, he's not looking at her and he's slightly rocking, actually conveyed a lot more about what he felt."

Andy had hesitated when Peter Jackson first asked him to play Kong. At the time, he was working on *The Lord of the Rings*, crawling around the motion-capture stage as Gollum, the computer-generated character hailed throughout the film industry as a breakthrough in CG animation.

"It was scary to go into another computer-generated character straight after Gollum," admits Andy. "But then Pete and Fran talked about where they wanted to go with the characterization. I became very excited about making him a creature that was driven by an actor's choices, although finally manifested in CG."

Andy and previsualization director/animation director Christian Rivers have talked through a sequence of action that will have Kong interacting with Ann and Jack when layered into the live-action footage. Andy performs the choreography. He wallops the benches and slashes at the foam cubes, sending them flying. His motion is swift, but his arms move with a heavy swing and there's an exaggerated bounce to his shoulders and head after each impact. Despite his too long legs, his too short arms, and his silver spots, he somehow, amazingly, looks like a gorilla.

"Gorillas have very swayed backs and very heavy bellies, so I'm bent and my bum is in the air for quite a lot of the time," he says. "I'm knuckle-walking. Gorillas use their knuckles to walk on. Sometimes we use arm extensions and put motion-capture dots on them, and that's fine if I'm just traveling, but not if I need to use my hands. They've got thick shoulder and neck muscles, so my head's slightly drooped below the shoulders. They've got a broad, bandy gait in the back legs. I've got huge weights on my forearms, across my thighs, and on my ankles, so that every movement has a momentum to it, because Kong is twenty-five feet tall. Not only does motion capture pick up shapes that you're doing, but it picks up impact and any incidental movement, any cough or breathing. It's a fantastically truthful tool."

For the last take of the day, Andy is given permission to go crazy. He roars. He thrashes. He thumps, swipes, and pounds. Christian Rivers screams at him, "They're attacking Ann! You're looking around for a place to put Ann! You put her in a safe place. They're attacking *you!* They're on your back!"

Andy falls onto his back and rolls frantically. He claws at his face, like a creature insane with pain and anger. It's as if he's caught up in a violent nightmare, swarmed by a mass of vicious bugs of his own imagining. The attack dies down. He pulls himself up to his full height, opens his mouth wide, beats his chest, and lets out a mighty roar. Then he collapses in a rag-doll heap onto a crash mat behind him.

Nobody else has breathed for the past two minutes. The motion-capture crew lets out a collective sigh and bursts into a spontaneous round of applause.

Peter Jackson, Naomi Watts, and Andy Serkis on set.

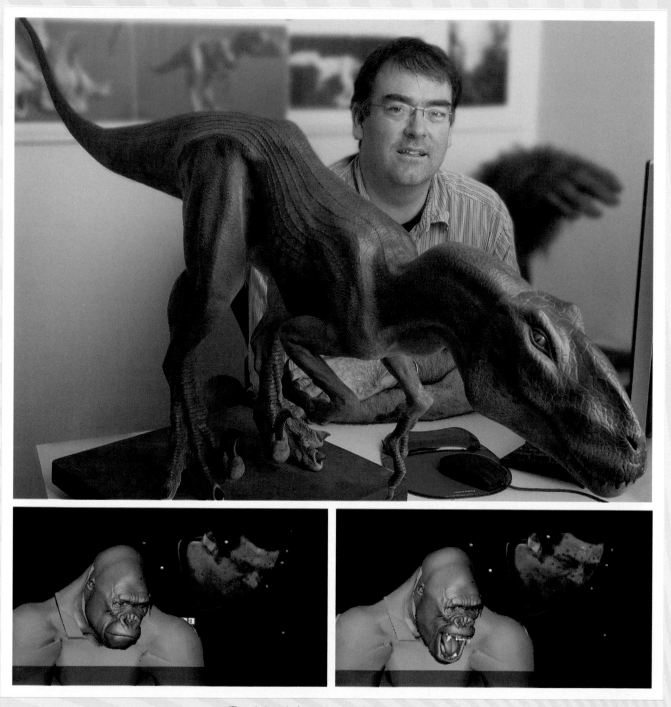

Top: Matt Aitken, pre-pro CG supervisor.
Below: Kong facial animation. Andy Serkis is performing facial motion capture, which is in turn driving the animation.

"For *The Lord of the Rings*, we didn't do any facial motion capture for Gollum at all. But we're building a system for Kong's facial animation where it can either be driven by an animator, or it can be driven by facial motion capture.

"For the facial animation system, we're building a whole lot of individual controls. Each one will do something like close the top eyelid or furrow the brow. There'll end up being more than ninety different controls like that, and an animator will use those individual controls to create a performance from Kong's face.

"With traditional facial motion capture, you have all those dots on Andy's face. On the computer replica of Andy, the dots are like a whole lot of individual magnets, so they drag the face around. And you can remap them so they fit onto Kong's face and drive Kong's face. So what you get is real Andy's face literally *driving* digital Kong's face.

"But obviously, Andy's a human and Kong's a gorilla. The physiology of the gorilla face is so different. Gorillas can open their jaws wide and their lips stretch right back, much more than a human's can. If Andy draws his lips back, the system will recognize that, but it won't just amplify Andy's movement. It'll say, 'I recognize this as Andy drawing his lips back, and what have I been taught that Kong does in this situation?'

"Some of the Kong facial and body motions will be key-framed, because he will be doing things that Andy can't do on a motion capture stage. Key-frame animation is created by posing the digital puppet at certain key frames in a shot. The animation software then interpolates the animation to move the puppet smoothly from key frame to key frame. But a lot of Kong's performance will be motion-captured. With motion capture, we get fantastic ambient movement—all these little twitches. There's a real sense of liveliness to it. It feels alive.

"Kong has to have a character and a story arc. That's what actors do. That's their job. It seems churlish to think that a bunch of computer people can do it just as well as an actor. Also, it's hard for Peter and Fran to direct a building full of fifty animators, but with Andy onstage, all that directing effort is focused on him and then comes through to us in a very focused fashion.

"With Gollum, the connection between live performer and digital character was purely shape-based. With Kong, it's based more on emotional states than a purely physical level. When the system recognizes that Andy's angry, it takes Kong to his version of angry. So we get the best of both worlds."

# PUTTING A FACE TO THE BEAST

## AS EXPLAINED BY MATT AITKEN, PRE-PRO CG SUPERVISOR

207

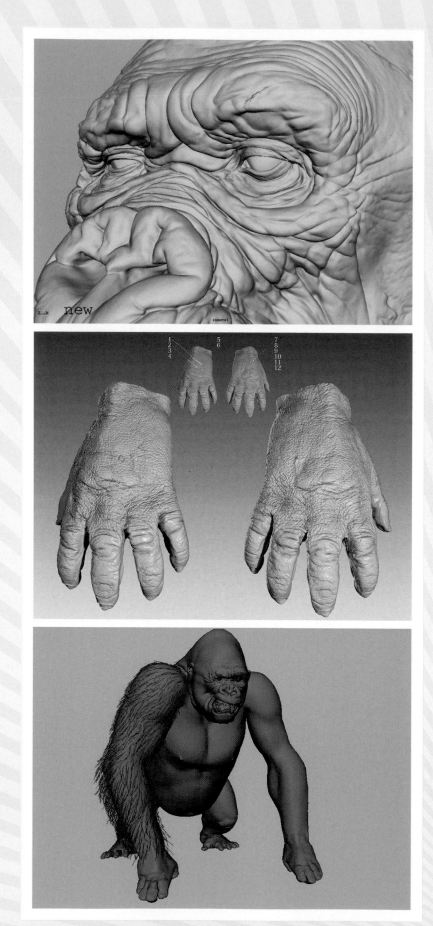

Top: Detail of Kong's facial geometry. Middle: Kong hand models. Bottom: Kong fur dynamic simulation.

Gollum was one of Weta Digital's greatest achievements during the making of *The Lord of the Rings* trilogy. The digital character impressed audiences and visual effects professionals alike. His motion-capture-led animation made for a memorable performance, which was made all the more believable by the astonishingly lifelike look of his skin.

"It was such an important breakthrough for us to figure out what makes skin look like skin—especially human skin," says *King Kong* senior visual effects supervisor Joe Letteri. "We created a technique called subsurface scattering to simulate translucency in the skin."

"Your face is not a flat color," explains Richard Taylor. "Light is passing through seven layers of corpuscles and then re-reflecting back out of the skin, giving a translucent effect. If I open my mouth, my mouth is not black. The inside of my nostrils are not black. They glow subtly with a pinkish glow, because light is penetrating the subsurface of my skin and then scattering, and it is that technique which we had been pursuing for many years.

"Joe Letteri saw a silicone puppet that Gino Acevedo had painted where all of our paint was added as a surface on top of the silicone, but still generated the impression of subsurface scattering. Gino is a totally traditional artist. Combine his skills

with digital artists and, in a matter of four months, we found a cohesive crossover that allowed us to come up with the technology that made Gollum's skin look real."

Weta Digital now applies that illusion of translucency to every creature they create: "No matter how tough or hidebound the skin, it is still skin," says Joe. "Just getting a little bit of that quality into the skin helps bring it that much more alive. Even Kong, under all the fur, and as old and scarred as he is, when you do see his skin, it still has to look like a real creature."

With Kong's fur, the visual effects team is moving beyond Gollum. "We've seen fur done very well in the past," says Joe, "What we're trying to do now is bring that life of the skin that we had in Gollum to the way we create fur. Some of those same properties are what makes hair or fur look as it does. It's really hard to put your finger on it and get the look of it right. There's a translucency to hair that we're trying to capture. And that'll work for any of the digital doubles that we have to create, as well as for the big guy."

For seven months now, a digital effects team has been totally engrossed in creating Kong's fur and skin. "We've got three guys doing fur," says Guy Williams, Kong CG supervisor. "One guy's doing the

# DIGITAL FUR AND SKIN

210

christian_head_10%

Kong fur in a work-in-progress stage.

Kong head fur in a work-in-progress stage.

legs, one's doing the back and the arms, and the other's doing the head. And we've got six guys doing textures, two or three writing shaders, which describe how surfaces should respond to light. We've been working on Kong since the dawn of time!" He laughs.

"Not just the fur—the whole look of Kong. He's been various different apes over time."

Guy delves into his computer and brings up video footage of an albino gorilla with an extraordinarily mobile and expressive face. "This is an ape by the name of Snowflake. Fran and Pete went to a zoo in Spain and spent a day looking at it and videotaping it. Snowflake was the only albino ape in captivity—spectacular-looking creature. Unfortunately he's passed away now. Pete initially loved the look of the character of Snowflake, because the skin on Snowflake was very baggy, very saggy. The face was almost human-looking—really baggy eyes and tons of folds in the face, and he seems to have a lot more range of expression in his face than other apes. So that was one of the main original designs with

Kong . . . and that's also one of the things that we're stepping back on now.

"Our second generation of Kong doesn't have half as many bags in the cheek region, and the brow is incredibly smooth compared to what Snowflake had, but there's still a lot of character there. Fran and animation want to maintain the ability to see the expression in Kong's eyes, so we're reducing the size of the brow back so they won't be so shadowed. Obviously Kong was never going to be an albino ape. We went towards gray-brown fur, and then it was decided that Kong was going to be a black ape, with white fur. It's a constant refinement process."

Kong needs to look like a real gorilla, but he also needs to look gargantuan—and it's not a matter of simply scaling him up. "We keep pinning a little Naomi Watts cutout in there beside Kong, just so you can get a sense of the scale," says Guy. "With the really coarse hair on an ape, by the time you scale it up so he's twenty-five feet tall, it would be a millimeter in width. So then, when you've got Naomi running her hands over it, it's not like she's running her hands through hair, it's like she's rubbing her hands through spaghetti. But if you take a twenty-five-feet-tall gorilla and put normal hair on it, it will look like a really soft plush toy, because the hair is too fine now in relationship to the size of the ape. That's one of the big things we keep waffling back and forth on—the width and the number of hairs. It's this weird scale thing that we keep chasing."

The color of Kong's eyes is also up for tweaking. "Real apes have a variety of different eyes. It's bizarre. Humans always have a white sclera area and a colored iris. We've got pictures of apes that have a black sclera and black iris, but we've seen some that have a deep creamy brown sclera with a really black iris. So we're trying to figure out which is the best-looking one. I'm leaning more towards darker myself, for the simple reason that you don't look at that and think there's a guy in an ape suit."

Having a twenty-five-foot Kong interacting with a normal-sized Naomi Watts means that he must be ultradetailed and extremely high resolution. "Whenever you see Naomi inside the digital Kong's hand, his thumb will be really large in frame," says Guy. "Kong is about four times the resolution of Gollum. We have to get a lot closer to parts of Kong than we ever had to on Gollum. We've painted all the pores on the skin, the really fine wrinkles, and we actually painted all the fingerprints, including on the palms and the thumb. That snaggletooth is about a foot and a half tall, and Naomi is going to be standing next to Kong's face a lot, so you're going to see that tooth jutting out. You wouldn't think a tooth would need so much detail." He laughs.

The good news is that the digital artists don't have to repaint all those details for each and every shot: "Once we've painted those maps, they're available—they never have to change. So we painted the fingerprints for his hand and we'll never paint them again."

The latest version of Kong's skin shows a shift from a leathery elephant-hide look to a more apelike, black, polished leather. "It's kind of cool," says Guy. "It looks like a fancy horse.

"One of Pete's constant driving factors is that Kong is an old ape and he has not lived a happy life. Everything wants to kill him and he doesn't really mind killing it back, so he's covered in all these really beautiful scars. We've been trying to get the character of those down. We have hero scars, where we'll cut the fur out in those areas. Other scars we might only see through the hair."

The Kong team has developed a series of texture maps that govern the behavior of Kong's skin, telling it where to be leathery, where it flexes more, where it is shiny, where dull or dirty, where moist. The skin on

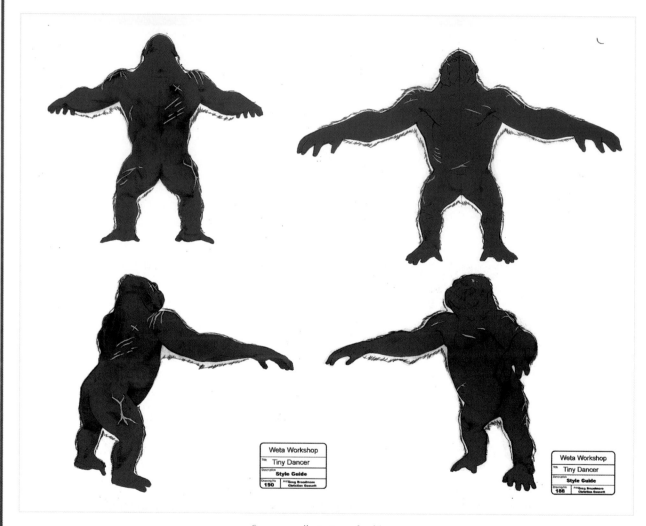

Scar map illustrations for Kong.

the back of the fingers will be more dull and leathery, the skin on the face more shiny and flexible, with wetness under the eyes and on the lips. The degree of subsurface scattering can be dialed up or down for greater translucency in the skin of the face, less in the skin of dusty hands.

Weta Digital's fur software was originally written for the digital doubles on *The Lord of the Rings*. "Basically, it detects a surface and you tell it to grow fur," says Guy. "Then we have to tell the fur how to behave once it comes off the surface—to wave around a little, for example, or to group into bigger clumps of fur. The amount of effort that goes into the creation of the fur is just staggering. Right now it still has a unifor-

mity to it. We're fighting to get it to look more organic.

"Kong has hairs on his arm that are over four feet long. It's like a horse's mane, but we don't want to make it as floppy as a horse's tail and we don't want to make it too stiff." Then there's getting the hair to move naturally in the wind, flicker with the impact of Kong's hands or feet hitting the ground, respond appropriately to light, with a peppering of white hairs among the black, and maybe some reddish highlights but not so much that he will turn red from the subsurface scattering of New York's dawn light . . . "One of the fun things about working in a place like this is that there is no end to the attention to detail," Guy says with a grin.

Final shot of Kong fur.

Film editor Jamie Selkirk.

Once upon a time, films were edited after all of the scenes had been shot. On *King Kong*, editing started before shooting had even begun.

Months before the cameras started rolling, action shots of dinosaurs, Kong, and biplanes flowed out of the previz department in the form of rough animations designed to communicate Peter Jackson's vision to the actors, film crew, and effects teams. In the cutting room, the previz shots were treated just as if they were live footage. "You'd end up with a cut scene of each action sequence," says film editor Jamie Selkirk, "and then that became the reference bible for how the scene was going to be shot."

First assistant editor Dave Birrell estimates that three million feet of film—hundreds of hours of footage—have been shot during the making of *King Kong*. As the footage comes in, a busy team of assistant editors has the daunting task of synchronizing pictures to sound and keeping tabs on every inch of it. "We have to log a ton of information," says Dave, "and then break everything down into shots, sort them, and categorize them . . . so that Jabez and Jamie can find everything that they need for a particular scene."

Jabez Olssen is the Avid operator. Although the movie was shot on 35mm film, the footage is scanned into digital form and the editors do their work on computer, using an Avid Adrenaline editing system. Jabez works in the cutting room, with Jamie Selkirk and Peter Jackson and occasionally Fran Walsh watching, discussing and making creative decisions.

Which take? Whose point of view? Is the storytelling clear? Does the pace feel right? Do the scenes flow seamlessly from one to the next? "The collaboration in the cutting room is quite essential," says Jamie, who has served as an editor or producer on every one of Peter's movies, starting with *Bad Taste* in 1987.

More often than not, the team is editing shots that are incomplete, with many layers of effects still to be added. "Once we've done a cut of a scene it all has to flow in about six different directions," says Jabez. "The assistant editors feed it to the sound department, visual effects, or miniatures people . . ."

As a result, it can take months to cut a single scene. "You get it cut, make it feel about right, and then send the information across to the digital facility so they can start animation," Jamie explains. "And then they send that back to us and we slightly adjust the scene, and then we send that information back, and they come back with newer shots, better shots. As the information grows, you keep fine-tuning to make it work better and better."

# MAKING THE CUT

Park Road Post atrium.

In Park Road Post's ADR stage, there is just one clue that Andy Serkis has been here this morning: the microphone is positioned at an unusually low angle.

"That's because when Andy's doing his Kong stuff," says supervising sound editor Mike Hopkins, "he's like this . . ." Mike hunches over and lets out a few Kongish grunts.

*ADR* stands for "automated dialogue replacement." On *King Kong*, just about every word of dialogue will need to be rerecorded, primarily because of Peter Jackson's demand for wind. "Anytime there's a noisy wind machine blowing on set," says Mike, "all the sound recorded on set is immediately no good." Meaning that, one by one, each of the actors will be coming to the postproduction facility to record their lines all over again.

Not that Andy has any actual lines when he's playing Kong. But he is, in a way, giving Kong a voice. "Andy is doing the motion capture which the animation of Kong is based on. We're also trying to have his vocal performance be the emotional heart and soul of the Kong vocal performance," says sound designer Ethan Van der Ryn. "In that sense it's a little bit like ADR recording, because we're bringing him back into the studio to do vocal performances for his character."

Mike and Ethan share the supervising-sound-editor duties on *King Kong*, with Mike taking responsibility for dialogue and Ethan spearheading effects and sound design. Neither was quite sure at first whether Andy's work this morning was an ADR session or an effects record session. "In the end we decided it was both," Mike says, laughing, "because it's an effects record session that we're treating like an ADR session."

The ADR recording stage at Park Road Post is laid out like a small movie theater, with a screen on one wall and a mixing desk at its center. It has a cozy, people-friendly feel, with big plush sofas and softly glowing table lamps. Special wall linings make the room acoustically neutral—if you clap your hands, the walls don't clap back.

The dialogue in a scene is replaced once the scene has been edited together. The actor stands at the microphone, watching the scene play back on the screen and listening to the original dialogue through a headset. To cue the actor, a white line runs across the screen. When it hits a certain point, the actor starts speaking. "We'll do a number of takes until I'm happy that we can make the words fit the mouth," says Mike, "and until whoever's directing the session is happy with the actual performance."

Lately, it has been Philippa Boyens directing the performances. Peter has been

POST SOUND

busy with shooting and editing, and Fran Walsh has been working with Andy on the mocap stage.

It used to be that, for ADR sessions, the actor stood alone in a small sound booth while the director and sound team worked in a separate control room. Mike prefers the new setup. "The actor is standing there, Philippa's on a couch, I'm on a chair at the side keeping notes, Chris is behind me at the workstation recording. We've got instant communication. You're not having to work through an intercom, which makes it so impersonal. This way, the actor is organically part of the process, actively involved in discussing the performance angles with the director."

For the actor, the challenge is not only to say each line in perfect sync with the original delivery, but also to recapture the emotional quality of the performance. "Some actors come in and they can do it like clockwork, and some come in and really struggle," says Mike. "Naomi Watts is one of the best technical actors I've worked with. She can stand there, watch the shot, you can see her working the scene, working her emotional center for the character, she gets herself into that zone, and bang, she does it, every take is just about perfect—in terms of sync and performance."

The spirit of action scenes can be particularly tough to recapture. "One of the most frequent comments from actors when they're doing ADR is 'How could I say that so fast on the day?' They're on set, in the moment, adrenaline's pumping, but get them back in the ADR stage afterwards, and unless they can really pump themselves back up to that same place again, they find it really hard."

Sometimes the sound team might record just the actor's breathing—for a running scene, for instance. "It depends on the actor you're working with, but where we can, we'll ask an actor to run on the spot really hard, and then plant their feet firmly on the ground, as if in concrete, and just do it with shoulder movement—puff, puff—so we can get that diaphragm, chest-cavity movement. Often we won't record every single running cue—we make up a grab bag of breaths, grunts, laughs, screams, for each character."

Andy's voice will be unrecognizable by the time the sound team has finished with it. For starters, it is being filtered through the Kongalizer, a specially designed sound rig that pitches the voice down to put it into the gorilla range. "Then we're taking that vocal performance back into the studio and processing it and editing it and shaping it to work with other animal sounds," says Ethan. "We've started merging Andy's voice with [that of] gorillas, different types of apes, some different big cats, lions, tigers."

Ethan says merging different sounds is not uncommon: "The objective is not to hear these different layers of sounds but to hear it as a single voice."

Developing a voice for Kong is an ongoing process of experimentation. At the moment, the thinking is to favor Andy's Kongalized voice for the more subtle, emotional moments, and augment it with larger roars and bellows when a more full-throated animal sound is required. "It's the big roars, the attack-roar moments, where so far it's feeling like we need to bring in other animals to give it more power and attack and strength."

Finding voices for the other creatures of Skull Island is also a matter of experimentation. "*Jurassic Park* set the bar," says Ethan. "*Jurassic Park* gave the general public a notion of what a dinosaur should sound like. To a certain extent, we have to live within that world, but we need to somehow change it a bit, take it in a slightly different direction.

"A lot of the traditional V-Rex sounds are very much in the Kong vocal range. When they fight with each other, we don't want there to be any confusion about who's roaring in pain and who's screaming at who. So we're going to have to twist the V-Rexes in what I'm hoping will be a more screechy, birdlike direction than the traditional T-Rexes, which are probably based around some big cats. But the V-Rexes are still on the drawing board. I think they will be a combination of some big cats and some big birds."

Ethan envisions Skull Island as teeming with life, conflict, and creepy-crawlies. "There's a lot we can do with sounds for things we can't see—all kinds of creepy stuff that we never see but we hear: 'Oh my God! What is out there?' I imagine we'll be hearing lots of things that we've never heard before. The people that are there are barely hanging on by their fingertips. They're at the end of their ropes and maybe they're half-crazy. I think some of the other life on that island can have that feel too."

Certainly there will be insects on Skull Island, so the sound design team has enlisted the aid of an expert—an eight-year-old entomologist. "He's a crazy bug collector," says Ethan with a laugh, "so we're setting it up for him to collect bugs for us to bring into the studio. We'll start by recording them and using those patterns to develop a palette of sounds for some of the insects—just so we can get an idea, even to stimulate our imaginations. I'm mostly thinking about the rhythms and patterns of wings and movement."

Some Maori wind instruments might also provide elements for wing beats: "You can get them to make all these different sort of fluttery vibrating sounds by blowing through them in different ways."

Then there are dead crabs—meat-filled, as opposed to empty shells. "You get some amazing sounds—just manipulating them very close to the mike. It makes a difference to have actual meat in the

*Peter Edge records sound effects for log impacts at Wainuioamata, Wellington.*

shells, to have a visceral action, to feel the mass and the guts and the gristle as part of the sound.

"So much of what we do is about experimenting," says Ethan. "You get some crazy prop and see what different sounds you can get out of it. And you may be thinking this is going to make a great sound for the insects, and you start blowing on it, and it makes some screech that turns out to be a good element for the bats. So much of the sound design creation that we do involves having the freedom to play."

Tomorrow, the team is scheduled to record a biplane—a 1920s-era Harvard. The biplanes in *King Kong* are Curtiss Helldivers, which no longer exist as working models. "While the Harvard isn't the exact same plane as in the shoot, it's the same motor, so it effectively makes the same sound."

The team will record the airplane's engine from on board and from a distance, as the pilot puts it through its paces. "The guys will make up a list of generic moves that we think we'll need," says Mike. "We've seen previz of the scene, so we can make a good stab at what the kind of moves will be. We'll get flybys and approaches, a fly past with a steep climb, flying high with a steep dive—all that stuff."

The taxi that Jack Driscoll races through the

streets and alleys of New York may prove to be a problem. "When they filmed that scene," says Ethan, "they put a souped-up engine into the old car body to get it to drive faster, so everything they recorded with that car is no good to us, because it's the wrong type of engine. So we have to go and rerecord it with a different car that has the right type of Model A engine in it, but can't drive fast enough to match the pictures they shot! So that's a challenge."

Ethan is keen to create some sound environments for *King Kong* that will flow around the audience—the sea, for instance, and wind. "I'm very intent on recording some of the environments in the quad format, so that we're hearing movement within a three-dimensional space, we're hearing it accurately as it's moving around us. For instance, we were recording the sounds of waves coming in and crashing on the shore, so we placed front microphones and rear microphones, to hear the waves moving correctly from the front to the back and then flowing back out.

"It's the same for winds, where we have winds swirling around us. Recording wind in foliage is actually very tricky, because it ends up just sounding like pink noise. It builds up in the trees and it's just like *shshshsh!* So we were trying to record in quad, with four distinct, discreet microphones—wind through bushes and trees and foliage, so we can get the sense of foliage moving around us in this three-dimensional space, to really put the audience there in the middle of the action."

For the sound team the movie is a kind of blank canvas. "We do everything from scratch, pretty much—from the footsteps to the body movements to all the different environments," says Ethan. "We go out into the world and figure out how to record all these different details, and then bring them back in

Recording the sound of water swelling against rocks in South Coast, Wellington.

here to the studio and manipulate them and edit them and weave them into this tapestry.

"If you think of all the different sounds that we weave together—the voices, the sound effects—all the different layers are going into creating this one voice of the sound track. Sometimes we want to hear the distinction between all the different elements, but there's other times where we want things to unify and we may be tuning them to elements in the music, so that they merge. That's a sound editor's job—weaving that whole tapestry of the sound track."

Recording sound effects for bullet impacts in Long Gully, Brooklyn, Wellington.

A shot of New York City from the final film.

There was never any chance that the New York scenes would be filmed in New York City itself. With the production based in Wellington, New Zealand, and the film set in the 1930s, filming in modern New York was simply not practical. The period setting, not to mention Kong's destructive rampage through the city's streets, required the creation of a digital Manhattan.

"New York is a big city," says Joe Letteri, evidently a master of understatement. As senior visual effects supervisor on *King Kong*, Joe was charged with the monumental task of creating a digital version of New York City to extend upward and outward from the few short streets built for the film's live-action scenes.

"The 1930s time and era are really important to the feel of the story," says Joe. "We want our city to look very natural and as true to New York in the thirties as possible, even to the point where we're trying to mimic all the coal smoke that would have hung in the air at the time. We wanted to capture the feel of what the city would have been like in that era that is different from today."

No stone, website, or accessible archive was left unturned in the search for photographs, newspapers, magazines, records, statistics, and other sources of information about 1930s New York.

"We started with the Empire State Building, since that's the focus of the climax of the film," says Joe. "We got blueprints for every floor of the Empire State Building and started building our digital Empire State Building from the blueprints, and we found some great old photos. We've learned quite a lot about this building over the past year."

Meanwhile, production designer Grant Major and the art department were planning the physical New York set, to be built a few miles away at Seaview, where the live-action scenes would be filmed.

"It's a pretty big set as far as back lots go. It's the biggest one I've ever seen," says Joe. Even so, it could only be one story high and three or four blocks wide. Anything above and beyond would be created digitally. And the vision was to create a 1930s city with endlessly long streets lined with towering buildings that rivaled the canyonlike architecture of Skull Island.

"We worked with Grant to plan both of these things together," says Joe. "We started with a big maquette of the Seaview set, on a huge table, maybe twice as wide as an average conference table. We spent a day with Peter, going through it with a camera, lining up photos of where he thought some of the key scenes and action would be.

"Then we did computer models of it.

# MAKING MANHATTAN

Plate from live-action filming of New York streets.

We built them in conjunction with what Grant was building, so we worked to the same blueprints for the ground floor and then started working on our extensions, going up and out. There are a few shots where we don't see off the top of the Seaview set, but not that many because Peter prefers wide-angle lenses or low angles."

The art department built detachable facades for some buildings so that the Seaview set could physically be altered for scenes taking place in different parts of the city. Changing the look of the digital upper floors of the buildings also adds to the illusion of multiple locations.

"The same block on set might represent three or four completely different areas of Manhattan," says Dan Lemmon, digital effects supervisor for the New York sequences. "We can modify our building extensions to give the feeling that this movie is happening all over New York." Just to prove it, he opens a computer file showing images of one Seaview building with two different upper-floor extensions—one textured with brick, the second textured with lighter stone. They do indeed look like different buildings.

"Here's one of the shots that we've been working on," he says as he pulls up a shot of Ann Darrow chasing Weston, the talent agent, across a New York Street. It is raw footage, looking exactly as it was filmed on set. Directly above the shop fronts is the Wellington sky, the pillars for the elevated train track support nothing but air, and the street dead-ends at a green screen. Dan also points out a mod-

The live-action plate with digital extension.

ern truck, a set surveyor, the production photographer, and an assistant director prepping an extra to walk into the scene. "The Steadicam operator had swung just a bit too far to one side," he says, "but this was the take Peter liked, so we're having to put additional elements over the top of these things to cover them up.

"You can see immediately the limits of the set. In the reflections in a lot of the windows you can see that the buildings only go one story up, so not only do we have to extend the buildings themselves, we have to extend their reflections. And it gets tricky because the glass is warped and the reflections kind of ripple as they go past.

"We're extending this block to go all the way down to give it that long feeling. The elevated train track and the elevated train have to be added, and of course we need to extend the shadows so it feels like they're walking underneath a track. Also, if the buildings were eight stories high, they would be casting a lot more shadows a lot further into the set, and that's something we have to work on. You really notice the lack of shadow in some shots, and others you can probably get away with it."

Dan shows a touched-up version of the shot, with the el tracks in place, the street extending into the distance, and the buildings several stories high. Suddenly the street seems fuller, more crowded. The setting, which had looked in the raw footage to be a moderately busy small town, has now been transformed into a bustling city with streets like canyons.

Top: Contemporary Manhattan data set, placed over a 1933 photograph.
Bottom: Data set backdated to 1933.

"We don't ever want to be in the position where Peter or someone comes up with a great idea and we can't do it because we weren't prepared for it," says senior visual effects supervisor Joe Letteri. "If you only build part of New York, it would be too limiting. From up above the Empire State Building, how could you say we only want to see parts of New York? So we just figured we had to come up with a way to build all of Manhattan."

CG supervisor Chris White figures he and his colleagues have built upward of ninety thousand unique buildings for New York City, out of 22 million separate components. It's considered by many at Weta Digital to be one of their greatest achievements on *King Kong*.

It would take nearly forever for a team of CG modelers to handcraft so many buildings complete with doors, windows, awnings, and other details. Says Joe, "We needed to write a piece of software that would build New York for us, let the computers do some of the work." Developing the main building blocks of the CityBot-Urban Development software took six months or so—led by Chris, who took a break in the middle to whisk back to the United States and complete his master of fine arts degree—plus another six months or so to get it working the way they wanted.

The digital effects team knew that

## ARCHITECTURAL NEW YORK

they wanted their version of the city to be historically as accurate as they could possibly make it, so the first step was to purchase a digital model of modern New York—a commercially available data set used by telecommunications companies, local government offices, and such. The model lacked detail, showing just the outlines of buildings and streets, with the buildings represented as simple geometric blocks and cubes.

The next step was to dig up statistical data on the age of each of the buildings and color-code them accordingly. Any building coded blue was built post-1933 and was therefore deleted. The model city's skyline flattened out as many of its high-rises vanished.

Meanwhile, researchers were tracking down every available photograph of 1930s New York. Finding aerial photography from the period was difficult, but thankfully not impossible. A treasure trove of 1930s aerial survey photos was unearthed. Anyone back in the 1930s who had the notion to go up in an airplane or a balloon and take a few shots of New York might be surprised to know how these pictures would be used some seventy years later.

"We lined our digital model up to all these 1933 photos, and then Alex Kramer and his modeling team started revising the data," says Chris. "Say they had a photo-

Left: 1933 photograph of New York City. Right: Digital New York placed over a period photograph.

graph from a certain view above the city. They would line up our three-dimensional city with that camera angle, and they would rebuild the cubes to match up with the photo. And then they would look at it from another camera view and see if it lined up there. So it's basically a form of tracing, from multiple views."

Once the team had a model of geometric shapes exactly matching the geometry of 1930s New York, the shapes needed to be dressed with surface details, such as windows and textures. Fifty-one landmark buildings with distinctive profiles, such as the Chrysler Building, Rockefeller Center, and the Empire State Building, were carefully handcrafted by the modelers to match whatever photos, blueprints, and specifications they could lay their hands on. The rest were dressed by the CityBot software designed by Chris.

The team studied the architecture of all the different kinds of buildings that existed in New York in 1933. "There's Italian, there's Federalist, there's colonial . . ." says Joe. "We build ourselves a library of digital architectural elements—windows, doors, ledges, park benches, chimneys, you name it. All the architectural elements and embellishments that we could get into a city, we built."

The CityBot software takes the basic geometric shapes of the 1933 New York model and dresses them with elements it chooses from the library. "We built our windows and such in different style groups," says Chris. "When the program is building a building, it tries to stay within a particular style for each particular building."

As I watch the CityBot do its thing, it seems like some kind of magic. An outline of the base of a building appears, as if drawn by an invisible hand. From each side sprouts a wall, growing upward from left to right to form a cube. Even before it is finished, a new base outline appears beside it and grows too. Details such as steps, doors, windows, and fasciae fill themselves in, followed by a texturing of brickwork. Within moments, there's a row of brownstones.

As much as possible, the program chooses from styles appropriate to each neighborhood. "For example, the Federalist style tends to be what we have downtown," says Chris. "There will be some discrepancies, but it's fairly close to the general shape and feel of the area as it was in the thirties.

"One of the issues we ran into was how to get the right color and texture for the buildings. We were randomly applying textures, so we'd have skyscrapers with bricks that didn't seem appropriate. One of our technical directors, Michael Baltazar, came up with a program that will allow us to look at a 1930s photograph and, based on the brightness of a building in the photograph, pick what would be an appropriate material to put on that building."

To weather down the freshly built New York, Chris and colleague Trina Roy have designed a pro-

Digital building weathering and aging elements.

gram that can simulate the effects of years of rainfall on the buildings. The simulation sends the digital equivalent of hundreds of thousands of water particles falling and sliding off the surfaces of the buildings. Wherever enough particles follow the same path, they leave a little trail of water staining.

"Peter also asked for snow on the city," says Chris. "Towards the end of the film, it's supposed to be after a snowfall, giving the city a frosty feel. If you just put in random pockets of snow, it doesn't feel like snow. Snow collects and builds up, and it piles up in some areas and it's cleared out of other areas. So we started to write programs that would allow us to place snow clouds within our 3D city, set a wind direction, and get snow to pour down and accumulate on the buildings. When it hits each surface, if there's enough of an angle, it slides off. If not, it collects naturally, builds up into piles, falls into gutters and traps, and piles up down on the roads. We can set it to snow on very large amounts of the city, so we're not dealing with every little building."

Building the whole of Manhattan, plus parts of Brooklyn and New Jersey, has given the production team the freedom to set up a camera anywhere in 1930s New York City they want. "We can fly above it, we can fly down to street level," says Joe Letteri. "There's no other place in the world you could shoot it that would give you that much scope. There's no city, no back lot, that would allow you to do what we can do in the digital realm. There's no other way to build New York in 1933."

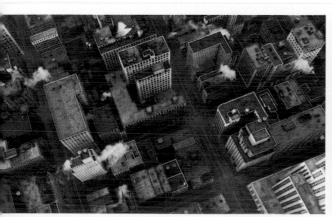

Left: Digital city without snow. Right: Digital city with snow.

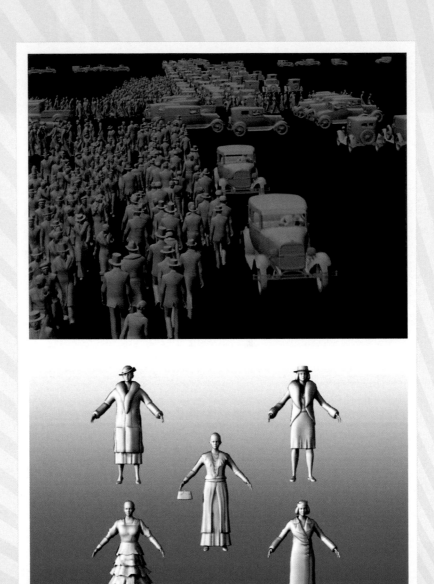

Top: Digital street crowd animated with Massive.
Bottom: Massive performers or "agents."

As New York busily builds itself, the artists at Weta Digital turn to the Massive task of populating its bustling streets with people and vehicles.

"We use Massive when there's too much going on for one person to sit down and individually animate every single guy," says Massive supervisor Jon Allitt, as he digs through computer files for a street scene.

Massive is the artificial-intelligence software Weta Digital uses for generating crowds. It was developed for *The Lord of the Rings*, to create hundreds of thousands of autonomous characters, called agents, who could battle each other as orcs or elves. For *King Kong*'s New York, the agents are less fantastical, being everyday people, but in some ways they are far more complex.

A digital New York street, cluttered with cars and pedestrians, appears on Jon's screen. "We start by building them a brain," he explains. "Each agent has its own brain, and they think for themselves. With *The Lord of the Rings* combat brain, the inputs are find a bad guy and start trying to hit him. For New York pedestrians, it's a little bit more vague, but it's more complicated because there are more situations that they have to cope with."

The pedestrians set off along the sidewalks. They walk, hurry, wander, loiter at corners, step around lampposts, pause at curbs, jaywalk, go in and out of buildings, look in shop windows, or stop for a shoe shine. They have each been given a complex set of rules, options, and objectives, but within those parameters they can respond to their environment and make their own choices. So, if one agent's objective is to get his shoes shined, but another agent has beaten him to the shoe-shine stand, he can choose whether to stop and wait or to pause, then walk on.

The agents are thick on the ground, but amazingly, none of them collide, either with their environment or with each other.

"It's all based on sound," says Jon. "These are all blind people with very acute hearing. We'll make a car sound different to a person. It's not a real noise, but the way that the agents are aware of it, it's like a sound. So the further away from it they are, it gets quieter."

Jon runs a crowd simulation designed to test how the pedestrians adjust to avoid collisions. In an empty space, two small crowds of digital pedestrians walk toward each other. As they meet and merge, the individuals within each crowd slow, side-step, jostle, squeeze through the gaps, perhaps fall into line behind an agent that has forged a path, and finally pick up pace again once the way ahead is clear.

The pedestrians can choose their

# MASSIVE TECHNOLOGY

moves from a library of specific actions modeled by actors and captured on the motion-capture stage. "When you watch a real crowd of people moving around, people are constantly taking half-size steps left and right to negotiate the pedestrian traffic," says Jon. "We captured lots of different walking actions, including people walking on a forty-five-degree angle or with their shoulders turned. As the agent is walking along, he'll think, 'I have to move a little bit left,' so we blend in a bit of one of those forty-five-degree actions to give a natural sidestepping motion. It's a case of putting yourself into this guy's shoes and saying, 'Okay, if someone's coming towards me but slightly to the left, which way should I go?' So then we put those kinds of rules into the brain."

Many shots of New York streets will have crowds of real actors in the foreground and digital people in the background, and their actions and clothing will need to match closely so that audiences will never notice the difference. During filming on the live-action New York set, hundreds of photographs were taken of the extras in their costumes, as reference for their digital counterparts. The Massive New Yorkers can choose how they are dressed from a library of muted colors, textures, and clothing styles consistent with the costuming in the live-action shots. Similarly, the photographers took pictures of the vehicles on set, from which the models department built up a library of cars, delivery vans, and taxis.

Jon demonstrates an early car simulation. The outline of a road appears on his computer screen, with neat rows of Model A Fords. "These cars have

Digital set extension, with foreground live action and background Massive agents.

232

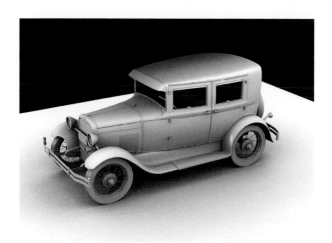

Automobile animated with Massive brain.

quite a simple brain, but they know to follow the road, not run into each other, and merge sensibly. We haven't quite got to the point of stopping for pedestrians yet, but that's going to come."

The cars proceed along the road in a politely law-abiding fashion. "The first thing these cars will all do is drive in perfectly straight lines, all perfectly spaced apart. The real world isn't perfectly ordered, so we've got to go in and jumble that up. We have a lot of ways of adding randomness to it—for instance, the cars will all get an initial speed, which is random."

Oddly enough, the cars drive their drivers. "The car and the driver are separate," says Jon. "The car will decide to change lanes, but it has to tell the driver to turn the steering wheel.

"We did a motion-capture session where we captured some drivers. . . . We can fold that into the brain as well, so, as the cars change lanes, the drivers will turn the steering wheel the correct way."

Each motion-captured action is added to what is called a motion tree, a carefully plotted network of interconnected nodes and branches. "For example," says Jon, "one node on the motion tree would be the action of someone sitting relaxed in a car seat. Then branching out from there, you'd have an action of him grabbing the steering wheel, turning the starter, and then an action of him putting it into gear, and then both hands on the wheel driving. From the re-laxed position, the only thing the agents can do is start driving or have a conversation with the person next to them while they're waiting for something to happen. While they've got both hands on the wheel, there's a variety of things they can do from that basic driving position, such as changing gear and turning the wheel. We have to plan all that carefully, so we can make sure each driver behaves sensibly.

"When we're building the brain, we're whittling away at the things we don't want the agents to do, and adding things in that we do want them to do," says Jon. "It's time-consuming, but worth it because, once we've got the brain fine-tuned, we can transfer it to different situations. We can put two hundred people on a footpath facing this way, two hundred people on a footpath facing that way, and they'll fig-ure out where they are and what they're supposed to be doing. If you need pedestrians in a shot, just give us the footpaths and we'll put the pedestrians down there, press the go button, and watch what happens."

Ann Darrow greets the dawn in New York City.

The film's final scenes atop New York's Empire State Building are set at dawn, a time when natural light subtly evolves from moment to moment. The decision to build the entire city of New York digitally gave the filmmakers not only the freedom to film any part of the city they might choose, but also complete control over the time of night or day.

"Since we have a complete 3D city, Peter can ask for whatever he wants in terms of lighting," says Chris White, designer of the New York CityBot software. "We're not locked down to some helicopter shots that we did, or some photographs. If Peter wants to make it look more dawn or more moody or more backlit, we can move the sun."

Dan Lemmon, digital effects supervisor for the New York sequences, has been working on the lighting for the Empire State Building scenes: "Peter and Andrew Lesnie, the director of photography, had requested to have [a] change in lighting as this sequence takes place. We wanted to make sure that we based it in reality—what the light in New York actually looks like at dawn—so we hired some photographers in New York to go up to the top of the Empire State Building and take panoramic photographs as the sun came up, from predawn all the way up to later in the morning."

Those photos now serve as reference for the sun's position in relation to the city and for its changing effect on the city's buildings. "The key light [the sunlight] in the early morning is very saturated, very orange," says Dan, "whereas the fill light [the sky light] is very blue. So you get this orange and blue contrast on the buildings, and that was something we wanted to get into our scene."

In much the same way as a theater lighting technician or director of photography can control the lighting on a physical set by placing lights and tweaking their color and intensity, the digital lighting team can place and control sources of light over their three-dimensional city and adjust them to achieve whatever lighting effect they need.

Dan opens a computer file showing a lighting test on the digital model of New York City: "We put Manhattan on a sort of a turntable and spun it around so we could see how our lighting is behaving and try to get that match to the reference photos." He gives Manhattan a demonstration spin. With the sun in a fixed position and the city spinning wildly, dawn light splashes orange over buildings, which quickly fade to blue as they revolve into shadow.

"On the particular day that they shot the photos, there weren't many clouds in

# LIGHTING A DIGITAL WORLD

235

Top and opposite: Digital New York with atmosphere and dawn lighting.

the sky," says Dan. "We're going to be having bi-planes in a big aerial battle, and in order to see that the planes are actually moving, you need clouds behind them to get that difference in motion." Happily, Wellington—home base for the production—boasts a plentiful supply of clouds. "We've had photographers here go out periodically and shoot vistas of different skies. This is one that we've been using for New York," Dan says, pulling up a sky shot with bits of Wellington harbor at the bottom of the frame. "We've chopped off the top bit of the clouds and we've put that in our New York sky environment, lined up the position of the sun, and that's what we're using as our baseline environment."

These days, New York is much cleaner than it

was in 1933. "They were burning coal for heat," says Dan. "There were a lot of coal fires, so it was a lot sootier and smokier. We had some great reference photos of 1930s New York, and with all the smoke in the city, you get these really interesting planes of light . . . that's one thing that we're working on now—getting a lot more of the smoke and that hazy, dirty feel.

"Of course, all the period photos are in black and white, and so people today don't associate vibrant colors with that era. But the dawn sequence is supposed to be really saturated, vibrant colors. We're working on striking a balance between that old-looking, smoky, period feel, and a present-day, bright, colorful kind of feel. There's a middle ground there somewhere."

Lens: 20mm  nsr_9200a_t01

Counter-clockwise: Digital damaged taxi. Destruction test for Kong's escape. Digital destruction of a Curtiss Helldiver.

Gray Horsfield specializes in destruction. "If it breaks, I've had something to do with it," he admits. "It's fun! I like breaking things, and on *Kong*, there's so much stuff to break."

New York buildings, for starters: "Kong jumps through walls, breaks glass, and the Empire State Building gets shredded by tracer fire. Plus, the army is firing tank shells at him, which of course miss and hit more buildings."

Then there is vehicular destruction: "Planes, trains, tanks, trucks, cars—most of which Kong picks up and throws around."

And, of course, rampaging dinosaurs: "Whole cliffs start collapsing under the weight of a herd of stampeding Brontosaurs—lots of rocks and rubble."

It would cost way too much to build so many items as miniatures and then blow them apart, so Gray, destruction supervisor, and his team, nicknamed the Bomb Squad, are developing software to enable them to destroy digital versions at the push of a few buttons.

"You don't want to have to digitally sculpt every one of those pieces of broken rock or glass by hand," he says. "We needed a programmable method of doing that."

He taps into his computer and runs a glass-breaking simulation: a bullet hole appears in a pane of CG glass, which cracks and flies apart in a spectacular shower of falling shards.

## BOMB SQUAD

"Anyone working on a shot with glass and bullets will be able to select their bullets, select their glass, apply the Bomb Squad's magic procedure, and then all this stuff happens," Gray says. "It's all based on standard real-world physics. The computer takes care of most of the physics stuff for you."

For Kong to break through a wall, Gray needs to know what is inside that wall, and how it is all held together. He then needs to reconstruct the wall, right down to the last digital nail, before he can simulate its destruction. "If you want the appropriate bits to detach and fly off in a realistic way, you've got to go in there and put the nails in the wood."

Getting it right according to the laws of physics is not the end of it. It has to *look* right: "You can't just shove something in front of Peter Jackson and say, 'There's your physically correct simulation of a biplane falling apart. I hope you like it.' He's likely to say, 'I want this wing to move over here.' So you need methods of changing where the break points are going to be. I can go in on the model and paint lines that I can get the software to follow as a crack propagation—I just paint a bunch of cracks and off it goes."

Gray's next job is to snap some trees. "Destroying organic shapes is infinitely more complex than planes and glass," he says happily. "That stuff is going to be hard."

Kong in his final moments.

When Peter Jackson, as a child growing up in New Zealand, first attempted to film *King Kong*'s Empire State Building sequence, his special effects techniques were not so very different from those used in the original *King Kong*.

Young Peter built a model of the Empire State Building and a simple stop-motion Kong and painted a bedsheet with a Manhattan skyline to pin up as a background. For the 1933 movie, a stop-motion Kong climbed a model Empire State Building in front of a sheet of glass with skyscrapers painted on it and, behind that, a painted backdrop of the Hudson River and shoreline. A small doll stood in for actress Fay Wray in the wider shots, and model biplanes circled Kong on wires. For closer shots of Ann, live-action shots of Fay Wray were back-projected onto a tiny screen positioned within the miniature setting.

Amost seventy years later, with a wealth of cutting-edge digital technology at his fingertips, the challenge for Peter is to create an Empire State Building sequence that will be as good as the original.

When *King Kong* came out in 1933, with its thrilling climactic scenes on top of the Empire State Building, the movie immediately found favor with audiences. "It was a smash success," says Peter. "It was the equivalent of *Star Wars* or *Jurassic Park*. It was audacious and outra-geous . . . a brilliant piece of storytelling."

The shock of the new made the film's final scenes especially powerful. "In 1933," says senior visual effects supervisor Joe Letteri, "the idea of seeing this big gorilla from the other side of the world was not a common thing. Mountain gorillas had only been discovered some thirty years before that, so these were big, unknown, almost mythological wild creatures at that time. . . .

"At the same time, we had the brand-new Empire State Building, which had just opened. Most people had never left the ground. Air travel and going up into very tall buildings wasn't common. So one of the brilliant things that the original *King Kong* did was it brought both of those worlds together. You have this beast that was king of his jungle lair come to the heart of civilization and rise to the top of the tallest building in the world, where you see this incredible vista. Those images were stunning and had a big effect on audiences at the time."

These days, wild creatures, airplane flights, and sweeping views from high places are not such a big deal. "We've all taken an elevator to the top of the Empire State Building, or we've seen photos," says Joe. "We take spectacular vistas for granted. We're so used to air travel being a comfortable thing for us. But if you climb into one of those biplanes, you realize

# THE TRAGIC END

Previz for Curtiss Helldivers' attack on Kong at the Empire State Building.

242

there's not much between you and the ground but a little bit of wood."

In faithfully re-creating an authentic 1930s cityscape—New York as today's audiences have never seen it—the visual effects team at Weta Digital is hoping to give audiences a glimmer of what 1930s audiences must have felt when they saw the Empire State Building sequence for the first time. "We wanted to bring people back to that era, when that clash of the two worlds was just happening for the first time," says Joe. "That's really the power of the story—this magnificent creature that is the last of his kind meeting civilization at its pinnacle. We're hoping to bring to audiences that sense of 'Wow, this is really amazing.'"

In Weta's digital New York, with the city's skyscrapers pared down to 1930s heights, the Empire State Building regains its stature as the tallest building in the world. "The Empire State Building is so much taller than anything else on the entire island," says Peter. "It stands out right in the middle like this huge needle. It's quite striking."

For Peter, making *King Kong* is the opportunity of a lifetime to re-create an iconic cinematic image for a new generation of filmgoers. "That black-and-white photograph of Kong on the Empire State Building swatting at planes, that's been in every book about the history of film that's been published in the last seventy years. By re-creating it we're tipping our hat towards an historic film moment."

Re-creating the sequence does not mean sticking slavishly to the original. The stop-motion Kong and two-dimensional painted backdrops of the 1933 movie constrained the pioneer filmmakers to static shots with the camera locked in selected positions, but Peter has a three-dimensional digital city and a digital Kong to play with.

"I'm able to do what they couldn't do in 1933, which is to move the camera around a whole lot more, and to have a lot more freedom with the camera angles. You've got aeroplanes wheeling and diving and swooping around the building, and I've used that a lot in the camera angles to try and give a very vertiginous and highly exhilarated version of the sequence."

A visit to the real Empire State Building, early in preproduction, kick-started the replicating of it for the movie. "We walked through it, measuring and photographing it," says production designer Grant Major. "We went to the upper observation deck, which is at the very top of the building, then climbed up above the observation deck to the machine level at the very top of the cone, and then went through a trapdoor and stood on the very, very top of the cone, as Ann did in the original film. At six o'clock on a fine New York day, it was freezing cold and very windy. It's not a very people-friendly place up there."

Structurally, the building is the same as it was when it was first built, but there have been many cosmetic changes. The very top of the building was originally intended to be an airport for dirigibles such as the ill-fated *Hindenburg*, with the upper observation deck conceived as a reception lounge for passengers, and what is now a television mast designed as a mooring mast for the airships, but that plan was scuttled by the high winds. "It's just a sea of microwave stations and radio masts up there now," says Grant. "Back then, it was quite a clean art deco shape. Fortunately, there's a quantity of archival photographs and movie footage of the time, so it's quite well recorded."

Most of the building as seen in the 2005 movie is a digital re-creation, but several small areas have been reproduced as physical sets. They include the entrance lobby, observation decks, stairways, exterior walkway and ladders, and, of course, the very tip of the cone where Kong fights the biplanes. "They're all completely different sets, and they're all based exactly one-to-one scale on the architectural drawings, measurements, and archival photographs of the Empire State Building," says Grant.

Some of the sets feature in the briefest of shots, yet have still been created with great attention to detail. For example, a lobby was built so that Adrien Brody, as Jack, could run through it and into the elevator. The lobby took weeks to paint because its wooden floor needed to look like marble.

"We had eight people painting it for around six weeks, full-time," says set finishing supervisor Kathryn Lim. "There are thirteen steps to painting marble. Every single step has to be sanded, because you want to have a mirror finish on it and it needs to look like it's got a lot of depth, that it is a beautiful organic piece of stone. There's a lot of blood, sweat, and tears that's gone into that marble."

The set for the top piece of the Empire State Building, the roof of the mast, was just a few meters across and set against a blue-screen background. It was built of medium-density fiberboard, prepacked with plugged-up bullet holes, plastered over, and painted to give it a smooth metal finish with not a bullet hole in sight. Between shots, the plugs could be popped out to reveal the holes.

Many of the bullet hits and ricochet effects on the building will be digital, but some strikes, such as those around Ann on the ladder, were created by the special effects team. "In reality," says Steve Ingram, special effects coordinator, "bullets going in just make a hole. But, in the film world, all bullet hits project outwards because visually the public expect more out of it. We put a squib, a little detonator, in the bullet hole, then we fill the hole with a mix of plasticine and silver dust. When you set the squib off, it blows out soft pieces that look like little shreds of metal but won't hurt anyone."

Shards of flying glass will be digital effects, but for some scenes the special effects team has made actor-friendly fake glass. "We made silicone glass which looks really real," says Steve. "You can crumble it with your fingers. It's for putting on actors. It doesn't matter if it falls down your sleeve or collar."

When Naomi Watts played Ann Darrow's final emotion-packed moments with the dying Kong, she was sitting on the tiniest of sets, surrounded by the film crew and a clutter of filmmaking paraphernalia. Stunt performers poked at her with huge blue-screened sausages, standing in for Kong's big, black, furry fingers. Andy Serkis stood above her on a snorkel lift, wearing a gorilla suit of sorts and grunting through the Kongalizer.

The biplanes were shot against blue screens in a separate studio. They juddered around on motion rigs, while a film light, standing in for the sun, swung past on a crane to give an impression of greater movement.

The completed Empire State Building sequence will involve a complex mixing and matching of live-

243

244

Curtiss Helldiver digital model.

An early frame from the Helldiver sequence.

action sets within a digital building, live-action and digital biplanes, special effects and digital destruction, live-action scenes shot out at the Seaview set, a vast digital city, a Wellington sky, actors, stunt doubles, digital doubles, and a digital Kong based on Andy's motion-captured performance. With computer wizardry, all the separate elements will seamlessly be woven together.

"The technology today is so incredible," says Peter. "Anything that you imagine is now possible on film. Anything that you want to see, you can create in the computer. In some respects, it is simpler to make movies now than it was ten years ago, because

you're not grappling with the 'How do I do that?' factor—which is good because I think that what's important now is to go back to the story and the characters."

Ultimately, of course, the Empire State Building sequence is not about bullet holes, blue sausage fingers, and digital buildings. It is about a wild creature trapped in a hostile alien world, an actress who is desperate to save him, a writer finding the courage to say that he loves her, and a filmmaker's reckless, shattered ambition. It is about Kong fighting the biplanes high above New York City, and the tragic bond between two lonely souls.

# ACKNOWLEDGMENTS

Thanks to:

Peter Jackson.

Gino Acevedo, Matt Aitken, Judy Alley, Jon Allitt, Malcolm Angell, John Baster, Jeremy Bennett, Danielle Birch, David Birrell, Jan Blenkin, Melissa Booth, Philippa Boyens, Greg Broadmore, Jed Brophy, Andrew Calder, Cindy Chang, Tanea Chapman, Julie Chebbi, Carolynne Cunningham, Gene DeMarco, Jason Docherty, Tony Drawbridge, Eddie Egan, Bette Einbinder, Ryk Fortuna, Richard Frances-Moore, Alex Funke, Eliza Godman, Dave Goodin, Beth Goss, Simon Hames, Ben Hawker, Jennifer Heddle, Chris Hennah, Dan Hennah, Belindalee Hope, Mike Hopkins, Gray Horsfield, Christopher Horvath, Bill Hunt, Gus Hunter, Steve Ingram, Helen Jorda, Peter King, Eric Leighton, Dan Lemmon, Joe Letteri, Kathryn Lim, Simon Lowe, Matt Madden, Grant Major, Clothilde Mayer, Sarah Milnes, Cynthia Modders, Eileen Moran, Ed Mulholland, Gayle Munro, Jabez Olssen, Phred Palmer, Christian Pearce, Hammond Peek, Dana Peters, Christian Rivers, Terry Ryan, Eric Saindon, Jennifer Sandberg, Atsushi Sato, Jamie Selkirk, Andy Serkis, Scott Shannon, Ben Snow, Chris Streeter, Amy Taylor, Richard Taylor, Ethan Van der Ryn, Paul Van Ommen, Ra Vincent, Nick Weir, Chris White, Fraser Wilkinson, Guy Williams, Jamie Wilson, Erik Winquist, Ben Wootten, Jake Yocum.